Smart Growth in a Changing World

Edited by Jonathan Barnett
With chapters by
Jonathan Barnett
F. Kaid Benfield
W. Paul Farmer
Shelley Poticha
Robert D. Yaro and Armando Carbonell

PLANNERS PRESS
AMERICAN PLANNING ASSOCIATION
Chicago, Illinois
Washington, D.C.

Copyright 2007 by the American Planning Association
122 S. Michigan Ave., Suite 1600, Chicago, IL 60603

ISBN (paperback): 1-932364-36-6 and 978-1-932364-36-1
ISBN (hardbound): 1-932364-37-4 and 978-1-932364-37-8

Library of Congress Control Number: 2006935997

Printed in the United States of America

Contents

CHAPTER

1

Smart Growth in a Changing World

Jonathan Barnett

The U.S. is in the midst of a growth crisis. It gets a little worse every day. Because it is a crisis created by our growing population, vibrant economy, high standard of living, rich natural resources, and abundant land, it is hard to perceive it as a problem. The danger is that we won't wake up to the true dimensions of what is happening until 15 or 20 years from now, when we will have wasted many of our national advantages, and when the costs of fixing our mistakes will far exceed the costs of anticipating and solving these problems today.

Our population is almost certain to grow by 50 percent between the U.S. Census in 2000 and the year 2050. There were 281 million people in the U.S. at the turn of the new century, and there are about 300 million today. By 2050 there will be between 419 million and 433 million. A 50 percent increase over 50 years does not sound so difficult to manage, and it wouldn't be if we could expect it to take place evenly across the whole country.

What is happening instead is that most of the growth is likely to be concentrated in nine multi-city regions, located in the Pacific Northwest, in coastal California around the Bay Area and between Los Angeles and San Diego, in the Intermountain West, in a triangular pattern in Texas, around Chicago, along the Northeast coast, across the Southeast from Raleigh through Atlanta to Birmingham, and in Florida. The population of Florida, a state that is almost all multi-city region, will double;

1

the Southeast multi-city region will grow by 150 percent. Only the Northeast is likely to grow at something like the national average rate; the other multi-city regions will grow much faster.

These predictions are based on a study conducted at the University of Pennsylvania in 2004, which projected the population of every county in the U.S., using a consistent methodology out to the year 2050. An explanation of the methodology and a tabulation of the most important statistics are provided in Chapter 2.

It is not a new discovery that cities and their adjacent metropolitan areas are growing together into multi-city regions, or that population growth is likely to be concentrated in such areas, nor is it necessarily a problem.

In 1915 Patrick Geddes in his book *Cities in Evolution* described how cities were growing together into what he called conurbations. He compared the spreading of London to the growth of a great coral reef, and discerned similar reef-like urban growths linking Manchester and Liverpool, and creating other groups of industrialized cities in England, Scotland, and Wales. He saw the Riviera in the south of France becoming a single urbanized resort, and he predicted that New York City would become linked to Philadelphia and Boston, forming "one vast city-line along the Atlantic Coast for five hundred miles."

Jean Gottmann verified Geddes's prediction in his study *Megalopolis: The Urbanized Northeastern Seaboard of the United States*, published in 1961. In that book Gottmann described continuous urbanization from metropolitan Boston to metropolitan Washington, D.C. Some people today would say that the same pattern now extends to Portland, Maine, on the north and Richmond, Virginia, on the south.

Multi-city regional patterns can also be observed in northern Europe, in Japan, and in the Pearl River and Shanghai regions in China.

THE PROBLEM IS SPRAWL, NOT MULTI-CITY GROWTH

The scope of our crisis can be read not in the total population projections for the multi-city regions in the U.S., but in the population projections by county. These show the number of counties that will become urbanized by 2025 and 2050. In the multi-city regions the number of urbanized counties will go from 444 to 797 by 2050, which means that almost as great an area is projected to become urbanized in the next four decades as has been urbanized in the whole history of these regions up to now. This is much more conversion of forest and farm land to houses and businesses than is warranted by the population increase itself. The problem is not that metropolitan areas are growing together, or that their population is increasing rapidly. The problem is the low density of new development in the U.S.

Low-density urban sprawl is the nation's normal growth pattern. While people often talk about sprawl as unplanned, most of it has been facilitated by long-established federal highway funding policies, mortgage guarantees, and tax subsidies, and almost all development has to meet local zoning, subdivision, and other codes. New buildings require permits; code changes and exceptions for a new development require hearings and actions by official bodies. New highways and other public works also go through a budgetary and review procedure.

It is hard to call something unplanned when it has been subjected to an extensive official approval process. Reforming such a deeply embedded system will not be easy. There will have to be changes in federal and state policies. Planners, government officials, and consultants who are working with outmoded codes and procedures will have to become agents of change as well.

Smart growth has emerged as the consensus term for alternatives to the current system of urban development. Smart growth has three basic elements: conservation of natural resources, encouragement of compact commercial and mixed use development, and walkable residential neighborhoods. There has been less discussion about a smart outcome regionally and nationally. Extending smart growth to multi-city regions means understanding natural systems at a regional scale and making certain that regional transportation initiatives such as highways, trains, and transit create a framework for compact development that is also planned with an understanding of regional ecology and sustainability.

WHY SPRAWL SHOULDN'T BE THE AMERICAN WAY

Some people assert that sprawl is part of the American way, the price we pay for competition and freedom of choice. It is true that right now we are still paying for sprawl, but we won't be able to keep on paying indefinitely. Kaid Benfield explores the consequences of the runaway American Dream in Chapter 3. He makes clear that current development patterns are already unsustainable and unaffordable; it is hard to imagine what the energy consumption, traffic congestion, air pollution, and erosion of the natural environment will be like in the multi-city regions if low-density urbanization, supported only by roads and highways, keeps on rolling across the landscape for several more decades. The statistical projections of urbanization for the multi-city regions are clearly unsustainable if they continue for the next 40 plus years. Long before they reach the projected extent, a compensating reaction will take place. The question is how far down the road to unsustainability we have to go.

BALANCED TRANSPORTATION
IS THE KEY TO SMART GROWTH

Sprawling growth patterns are hardly the right way to foster competition and freedom of choice. Inefficient urbanization imposes costs on living and doing business: fuel costs, travel delays, water shortages, unhealthy pollution, destruction of the natural ecology, overextended infrastructure. We now live in a global economy. If we wish to remain competitive, we need to keep an eye on how our competitors are dealing with comparable problems. The big difference, as discussed by Shelley Poticha in Chapter 4, is that other countries with multi-city regions have balanced transportation systems that include high-speed rail connecting urban centers, plus local transit systems. It is not that these countries lack highways and airports; rather, they have a transportation system that allows people to select the mode of transportation most suited to the trip they want to make.

In congested urban centers, it is better to use transit for short trips than to sit in traffic on highways and local streets—and then to hunt for a parking space. However, the transit has to be frequent and provide comfortable accommodations. For trips of less than 400 or 500 miles between urban centers, a high-speed train can produce better door-to-door travel times than either highways or airplanes, but it has to be a reliable service, and it has to average at least 75 miles per hour and preferably a lot more.

Chapter 4 begins with a round-up of current plans for high-speed rail in the U.S. The map of high-speed rail routes promoted by the Federal Railway Administration corresponds closely to the multi-city regions. The nation is too large for rail to be the sole mode of choice from one multi-city region to another. But rail may often be the best way to travel within the multi-city regions, even at the relatively low average speeds being planned for U.S. railroads, which, except in California, are expected to be far slower than the trains already in operation in Europe and Japan.

Skeptics in the U.S. keep saying that we are never going to get Americans to give up their cars. But a balanced transportation system does not mean giving up automobiles. People are riding the new light-rail systems around the country in unexpectedly large numbers. As Shelley Poticha points out, an important impetus for high-speed rail is not getting people out of their cars but giving them an alternative to airplanes. Close to half the airline flights at major airports are for shorter trips that could be made more efficiently by high-speed rail. Some of the money set aside for costly and controversial new runways could be used for rail improvements instead.

DEMONSTRATIONS OF SMART GROWTH POLICIES

Chapter 5 is a case study demonstrating the potential positive results of regional balanced transportation and environmental conservation in the seven-county Orlando region in Florida. The study, done at the University of Pennsylvania, made population projections to 2050 and then, using computer programs, showed how the projected population is likely to be translated into land development following current policies and densities.

Then an alternative was prepared using the same projections and computer programs, but with new assumptions about stronger environmental protection measures and a balanced transportation system. It turns out that the alternative is both better and cheaper. Much more of the natural environment is preserved, and the costs of land acquisition for preservation—and for high-speed rail and transit—are more than offset by *not* spending for infrastructure that would support more sprawl. Nor does this alternative mean a big change in lifestyle for people who like the way things are now. Despite increased density near rail and transit stops, much of region would continue as it is today.

Chapter 6 is a case study, also prepared at the University of Pennsylvania, which looks at trends and alternatives for the Northeast Megalopolis. Again, computer programs were used to map the damaging effect of translating population increase into further sprawl. Unlike the Orlando area, some parts of the Northeast are growing far more than others. The study estimates that no new urbanization would be needed in the region at all if the new population could be accommodated using vacant or underused land in the region's older, bypassed communities.

SMART GROWTH AND THE NATURAL ENVIRONMENT

Chapter 7 examines the concerns highlighted by Hurricanes Katrina and Rita in 2005. Climate change is making hurricanes and other storm events more severe and appears to be changing rainfall patterns in ways that threaten the water resources of some major cities. Rising sea levels mean that development in low-lying areas along coasts needs to be protected from storm surges. Development in some shoreline locations will become increasingly impractical. Wildfires seem to be increasing as well, possibly as the result of earlier spring thaws and longer dry seasons. Increasing urbanization makes the potential disasters from hurricanes, floods, and fires more severe.

There is also potential disaster from earthquakes, a problem well understood on the West Coast, but less familiar to people in the Salt Lake City, Memphis, Boston, and Charleston regions, which may be equally at risk. These issues all have to be considered in planning for future growth.

Even with strong regional growth policies in place, most of the decisions about development will still be made by local governments, the guardians not just of planning policy but of effective urban design. Chapter 8 describes how local smart-growth and urban design policies can operate within the larger multi-regional context, particularly in conserving the natural landscape, promoting walkability in special districts and residential neighborhoods, and transforming cities and regions into designed environments.

WHERE WE GO FROM HERE

The concluding chapter, by Paul Farmer, the Executive Director and CEO of the American Planning Association, discusses the need for federal smart growth policies and the role that planners need to play in devising and implementing them.

2

What Are the Nation's Future Growth Trends?

Jonathan Barnett[1]

According to the U.S. Census, in 2000 there were 281,421,906 people living in the 50 states. In 2004 the Census Bureau released an estimate of the U.S. population for the year 2050 of 419,854,000, almost a 50 percent increase. If we think we have growth management problems now, what will be the effect of another 140 million people? A research project at the University of Pennsylvania conducted in 2004 sought to describe the impact of this future population on current metropolitan development trends, estimating both population growth in cities across the country and the amount of additional urbanization likely to take place. At the time we began our research, the U.S Census Bureau had not released its projection of total U.S. population for 2050. There were also gaps in census projections for counties and in national projections for 2025. A second assumption, that we would be able to correlate information from the various metropolitan planning organizations around the country, also turned out to be overly optimistic. Not every M.P.O. does population projections; those that do make their projections for a variety of time periods, with a variety of methodologies.

HOW THE ESTIMATES WERE DONE

As a consistent set of estimates of population growth by county was essential, we turned to a convenient and affordable commercial data service, Woods and Poole Economics, Inc., using the company's 2002

Complete Economic and Data Source. It is a compilation of regional data and long-range projections for the entire nation, comprising all regions, states, metropolitan statistical areas, and counties for the years 1969 through 2025. Projections for all counties in the U.S. are done simultaneously so that activity forecast for one county will affect growth and decline in other counties. Forecasts of employment are made first by using an export base analysis, which examines the domestic basic sectors (agriculture, mining, manufacturing, and government) that are linked closely to the national economy, and then determines the other employment sectors. Changes in international exports are not included in the model. All other projections (earnings, population) are based on the employment opportunities.

The Woods and Poole data gave us our consistent estimates for population growth by county to 2025. Projecting to 2050 is obviously more speculative. To show metropolitan trends to 2050, we determined the rate of change in each county between 2000 and 2025 from the Woods and Poole dataset and then calculated a straight line trend for each county from 2025 to 2050 based on the rate of change from 2000 to 2025. In the spring of 2004, towards the end of our research, the U.S. Census Bureau issued their 2050 U.S. population projection of 419.4 million, but no state or county projections. The Penn 2050 population projection for the whole U.S. is 432.9 million. We take this variation of about three percent as confirmation that our straight line projections by county to 2050, while somewhat rough, produce a result that is close to the best available estimates. Of course, projections of current trends do not account for improvements in growth policy, innovations in technology, natural disasters, or wars, among other factors that would alter trends.

To our knowledge, these national population projections to 2050 are currently the only ones that extend to 2050 for every county, and thus permit consistent projections for all metropolitan areas.

GROWTH WILL VARY ACROSS THE U.S.

A 50 percent increase nationally does not mean uniform growth. At the state level, the figures vary widely. California is projected to grow from a population of 34 million in 2000 to almost 55 million in 2050, or more than 60 percent. West Virginia, on the other hand, is projected to grow from 1.8 million people in 2000 to just over two million in 2050, or 11 percent. Florida is expected to increase from 16 million to over

30 million—or more than 87 percent—while Nebraska's numbers are 1.7 million to 2.4 million, or around 40 percent.

THE MULTI-CITY REGIONS

The big revelation from these projections is not in the state figures, striking as they are, but in the dominance of nine rapidly growing multi-city regions, which we are calling the East Coast Megalopolis, the Pacific Northwest Multi-City Region, the Bay Area Multi-City Region, the Southern California Multi-City Region, the Intermountain Multi-City Region, the Texas Triangle, the Mid-West Multi-City Region, the Florida Multi-City Region, and the South East Multi-City Region.

This growth takes two forms: the overall increase in population in these multi-city regions and the increase in the number of counties that become predominantly urbanized between 2000 and 2050, using the U.S. Census definition of urbanization as an area that has a population of at least 50,000, at a density of more than 1,000 persons per square mile. The increasing number of urbanized counties gives a rough picture of the geographic expansion of urban areas up to 2050.

The most familiar of these multi-city regions is the East Coast Megalopolis. Geographer Jean Gottman (who coined the word "megalopolis" from the Greek words for big and city) identified the trends creating a megalopolis in the late 1950s. The Boston-to-Washington portion of the East Coast megalopolis is projected to grow from a population of 48.7 million in 2000 to 71 million by 2050, an increase of more than 45 percent, which is less than the national growth average. However, the number of urbanized counties in the region increases from 109 to 159.

The rapidly emerging Southeast Multi-City Region, stretching from Birmingham, Alabama, to the Raleigh-Durham-Chapel Hill area of North Carolina, is projected to grow from about 13.5 million people in 2000 to almost 34 million by 2050, an increase of about 150 percent. The number of urbanized counties in this multi-city region could grow from 87 to 196.

The Multi-City Region in the Pacific Northwest is projected to have an 83 percent increase in population by 2050 and an increase in the number of urbanized counties from 17 to 24.

The Bay Area Multi-City Region's population is projected to grow by more than 100 percent and its urbanized counties to almost double, from 20 to 38.

Multi-City Regions	2000		2025 PROJECTIONS		2050 PROJECTIONS		% CHANGE
	Population	Urbanized Counties	Population	Urbanized Counties	Population	Urbanized Counties	Population
East Coast Megalopolis	48,682,328	109	58,006,606	124	70,904,064	159	46%
Southeast Multi-City Region (Birmingham, AL to Raleigh/ Durham/Chapel Hill, NC)	13,487,334	87	21,097,869	123	33,667,010	196	150%
Pacific Northwest Multi-City Region	6,444,187	17	9,208,909	20	11,786,812	24	83%
Bay Area Multi-City Region	10,639,417	20	14,561,070	22	21,544,898	38	103%
Southern California Multi-City Region	19,905,624	8	25,363,501	8	30,931,407	9	55%
Intermountain Multi-City Region							
Denver	3,591,614	11	5,195,247	13	6,846,408	16	91%
Salt Lake City	1,843,286	6	2,877,592	7	4,195,167	13	128%
Texas Triangle (San Antonio, Austin, Dallas, Fort Worth and Houston)	13,134,311	27	20,170,467	35	28,544,958	62	117%
Mid-West Multi-City Region	44,157,882	129	52,930,123	159	71,484,594	239	62%
Florida Multi-City Region	14,027,512	30	20,442,400	30	27,651,083	41	97%
Multi-City Regions Total	175,913,495	444	229,853,784	541	307,556,401	797	75%
(% of U.S. Population)	62%		71%		71%		

Fig. 2-1: Summary of population increases and the increases in urbanized counties for nine multi-city regions between 2000 and 2050.

The Southern California Multi-City Region, which includes the Los Angeles and San Diego metropolitan areas, is projected to have a population growth of about 55 percent. Only one additional urbanized county (Imperial County) is expected to emerge, reflecting the large size of counties in this region and the sprawling development already taking place there.

The Intermountain Multi-City region is made up of two separate clusters, those around Salt Lake City and Denver. We project that population in Salt Lake City's portion of the multi-city region will grow by 128 percent and Denver's portion by 91 percent. Urbanized counties related to Salt Lake City are likely to go from six to 13, while those related to Denver could increase from 11 to 16.

The Texas Triangle Multi-City Region, which includes San Antonio, Austin, Dallas, Fort Worth, and Houston, is projected to have population growth of 117 percent, with urbanized counties going from 27 to 62.

The network of cities separated by agricultural areas that make up what we are calling the Mid-West Multi-City Region could see an average population growth of about 62 percent, and the number of urbanized counties is likely to go from 129 to 239.

The Florida Multi-City Region is projected to grow by more than 97 percent by 2050, with the number of urbanized counties going from 30 to 41.

And the amazing Southeast Multi-City Region is projected to grow by 150 percent, three times faster than the country as a whole, with the number of urbanized counties going from 87 to 196.

These changes in urbanization are summarized in Figure 2-1.

The nine multi-city regions already have a dominant role in the U.S., and this role will increase substantially by 2050. Altogether, we project that 307.6 million people—or 71 percent of the total U.S. population—will live in these multi-city regions in 2050. Nearly 176 million people lived in these areas in 2000, equivalent to 62 percent of the year 2000 population. We are predicting that the multi-city regions will increase in population by 75 percent. In the aggregate, these regions appear likely to grow about 50 percent faster than the U.S. as a whole.

The most telling prediction about the multi-city regions is the almost 100 additional counties that will become urbanized by 2025 with a total of 797 urbanized counties projected by 2050. There were 444 urbanized counties in the nine multi-city regions in 2000.

MULTI-CITY REGIONS AND GLOBAL TRENDS

Multi-city regions are cropping up in other developed nations, too. London, Paris, Milan, Munich, and Hamburg have been said to form the corners of a pentagon that encloses a high proportion of the economic activity of the European Union. A more specific geographic interpretation links London to Paris, Brussels, the cities of the Netherlands, and the German cities in the northern Rhine valley. In this interpretation, Hamburg is part of a multi-city region that includes Berlin, Warsaw, and Copenhagen. Copenhagen, in turn, is part of a continuous urban system that links to Stockholm, Helsinki, and possibly St. Petersburg.

Madrid, Lisbon, and Seville are part of a linked multi-city region on the Iberian peninsula. Barcelona can be seen as linked to Toulouse, Marseilles, Lyon, the rest of the French Riviera, and Genoa. Munich, Vienna, Prague, and Venice may be parts of another incipient multi-city region.

Japan from Tokyo south and west to Kyushu can be seen to be a multi-city region connected by high-speed train service. The Pearl River Delta in China, encompassing cities from Guangzhou to Hong Kong and including Dongguan, Shenzhen, Zhongshan, and Macau, is becoming one economic region. The cities between Nanjing and Shanghai, including Wuxi and Suzhou, are becoming an economic region that can also be understood to include Hangzhou.

The south and east coast of Australia from Melbourne to Sydney and including Canberra is also an incipient multi-city region, possibly extending to Adelaide and up to Brisbane and the Gold Coast.

THE GEOGRAPHIC CONSEQUENCES
OF POPULATION GROWTH

In Europe, Japan, and many other parts of the world, the growth of multi-city regions is being managed by government policies that restrict development of historic and environmentally sensitive areas, protect farmland, and center development around stations on rail transportation systems. In the U.S., most of the urbanization predicted for counties around the multi-city regions will be supported only by highways and local roads and there will be few protections for unurbanized land. There is likely to be an explosion of low-density development if population predictions are fulfilled and urbanization follows current trends.

The switches from unurbanized to urbanized at the county level do not give a true geographic picture because, while a county may become urbanized statistically, this does not mean that all the land area in the county has been urbanized. We need a way to describe the effect of increased population on the multi-city regions in the U.S. A map of urbanization that relies on county boundaries would overstate the problem, particularly in places like the Southwest and West, where county boundaries are much larger than they are elsewhere in the nation.

The 2000 Census gives us population by block groups, which is a fine enough grain to produce an accurate geographic picture. So a map of U.S. urbanization by block groups is a good starting point. Notice how influential the interstate highway system has been in the creation of multi-city regions. [Figure 2-2]

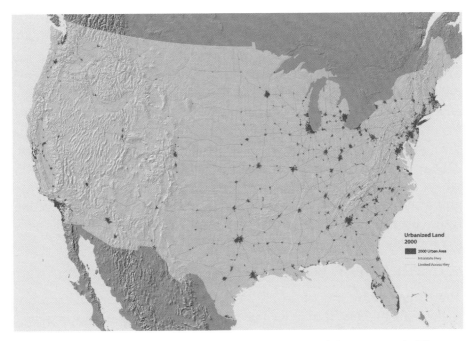

Fig. 2-2: Map shows urbanized areas of the U.S. as of the year 2000. The connecting lines are the interstate highway system, which has clearly been a major force in directing urban growth.

Raster GIS technology can translate the Woods and Poole county data for 2025 and the student-derived county projections from the Woods and Poole data for 2050 to create maps of urbanization in 2025 and 2050. These maps, while far more accurate than maps based only on county boundaries, are not completely accurate computer simulations because existing population density and household size vary across the U.S. Instead, these maps are descriptions of potential development made with the aid of the computer. Much more place-specific growth projections generated through computer technology are shown for the seven-county Orlando region in Chapter 5 and for the Northeast Megalopolis in Chapter 6.

The Penn maps are based on two assumptions. First, that population growth will result in urbanization outward from the urbanized areas shown in the year 2000 maps. Second, that the amount of urbanization shown in the map will be proportional to the population growth projected for each county, but its geographic distribution within each county should be shown in terms of an impedance model related to previous development rather than to the county boundaries. This model does not take into account growth boundaries, such as those in force around Portland, Oregon. It also does not take account of the influence of geographic barriers. On the other hand, it postulates an outward development pattern that does not fully take into account the leap-frog effect when development bypasses jurisdictions that are not receptive to new development and moves on to those that are. So in some places the map may overstate urbanization, but in others it may understate it.

Of course, the maps are only as good as the population predictions on which they are based. The 2025 maps, based on professional demographic projections, are thus likely to be a more accurate portrait of the future than the 2050 maps based on straight line extrapolations. [Figures 2-3 and 2-4]

THE MAPS PORTRAY AN UNSUSTAINABLE FUTURE

These maps show sprawl problems greatly intensified by 2025 and unsustainable by 2050. It may well be that the land-use patterns predicted in the maps cannot happen, because their inherent inefficiency will cause compensating events to take place long before development reaches the geographic extension shown in the maps.

Twenty-nine percent of the population in 2050 is expected to live in locations other than the nine multi-city regions described in this chapter, but growth pressures supported only by automobile transportation are likely to produce comparable patterns in these other areas. The multi-centric regions around Phoenix, Detroit, northern Ohio, and Pittsburgh also show up in the Penn national population model, as do other areas defined as urban by the Census in 2000, and the projections and related maps cover all urbanized areas and not just the nine multi-city

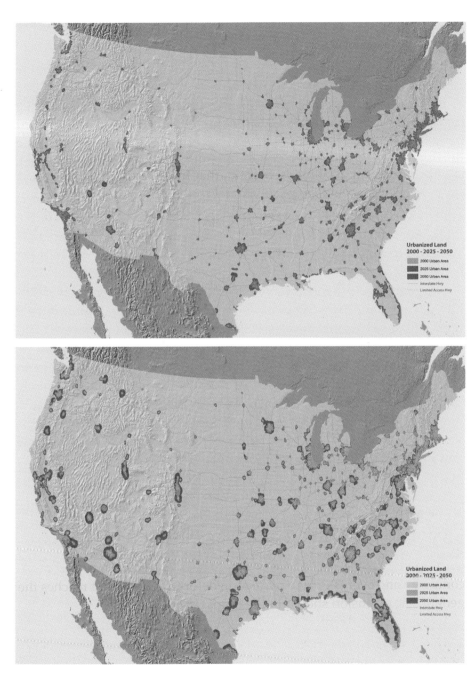

Figs. 2-3, 2-4: These maps are projections, not predictions, as the development pattern shown is unsustainable: (top) development within counties projected to become urbanized by 2025; (below) additional counties projected to become urbanized between 2025 and 2050. The sooner there is a reaction against current growth trends, the less public and private money will have been wasted.

regions. The U.S. Census also mentions what it calls micropolitan areas, defined as towns or cities with populations between 10,000 and 50,000; 50,000 is the Census Bureau's threshold for an urbanized region. Some 28 million people, or 10 percent of the nation's population in 2000, live in these micropolitan areas. These places are becoming an alternative for people who want urban resources and services, but who also want to escape the pressures and inefficiencies of the multi-city regions. The micropolitan development patterns don't show up in the Penn model, but they have been described as being as decentralized as larger city regions, with the original small town or city surrounded by the same kind of low-density urbanization that is found in the outer areas of the multi-city region. Even rural communities with less than 10,000 people are likely to exhibit decentralized development if any new investment is taking place at all.

The continued urbanization of the counties surrounding today's rapidly growing multi-city regions, as predicted in the population projections, will be a national disaster if growth follows the current trend and takes place without conservation policies and is supported only by roads and highways. Kaid Benfield in the next chapter describes in detail what is wrong with current urban development. We are unlikely to get to 2050 without a national consensus that things are going badly wrong, but every year spent making continued investments in what is already a failing development pattern will make the problems worse and more difficult to correct.

NOTES

1.   The population projections, maps, and other research in this chapter were prepared during a studio at the University of Pennsylvania in the spring of 2004 under the direction of professors Jonathan Barnett, Robert Yaro, and Armando Carbonell. Suchitra Sanagavarapu took the lead in the statistical analysis and projections, Eric McAfee devised the graphic modeling technique, and Kyle Gradinger created the graphic presentation for the maps. The other participants were: Laureen Boles, Lee Farmer, Joshua Gelfman, Maria Geisemann, Atara Margolies, Jennifer Posner, Felicia Roff, Joseph Savage, Leah Wright, Christine Wu, and Oliver Yu. The findings concerning multi-city regions were discussed at a working session at the Institute for Community Studies in London. The whole studio traveled to London to meet with European planning experts Sir Peter Hall, Prof. Andreas Faludi, Alfonso Vegara, and Vincent Goodstadt. Mark Pisano, executive director of the Southern California Association of Governments, also participated in this discussion.

3

The Runaway American Dream

F. Kaid Benfield[1]

In the opening line to his epic "Born to Run," Bruce Springsteen rumbles the phrase "runaway American Dream" to evoke a spirit of youthful restlessness and a yearning to escape one's circumstances, to change. In a sense, Springsteen's American Dream is not that different from the one that immigrants have long pursued: seeking and embracing the land of opportunity to improve their circumstances, to make progress. Writings about land development and planning often invoke the phrase to include home ownership, although owning one's home is but one part of the larger vision of success and comfort. At its essence, the American Dream is about progress, improving one's circumstances, about opportunity for succeeding generations to be more comfortable and more prosperous than their forebears.

Is that broader American Dream, the one of immigrants and new generations, running away from us? The quick answer might suggest that it is not, for the U.S. has always been and remains a nation of opportunity and progress. While our progress has taken many forms, we have long been on a path of growth, of moving forward. Today, at the beginning of the twenty-first century, we have a larger population and a larger economy than ever before. By many measures, those of us fortunate to be alive now are enjoying a remarkable quality of life, one with substantially more comfort and opportunity than our ancestors did.

Or are we? The fruits of progress have not been distributed evenly, as it turns out. Has progress for some come at others' expense? And, even for those of us who have prospered, can our prosperity be sustained? Will our children be able to reap the benefits of the American Dream?

The answers to these questions are complex and elusive. Many factors contribute to our sense of well-being and our ability to remain strong as a nation, as an economy, as a people. And more and more Americans are coming to challenge the assumption that our path of progress is inevitable. Many of us look around and are more unsettled than reassured by what we see, by the products of the changes we have wrought.

Unfortunately, we have good reason to be concerned. The patterns and projections of growth laid out in the preceding chapter would give one pause even without additional information. But when we examine them in the context of their consequences—of the facts and trends concerning the impacts of development patterns on our environment, economy, and society—it becomes clear that we can and must do better if we are to enjoy true progress, and if our great regions are to remain viable and strong in an increasingly competitive global economy.

FROM SEA TO SHINING SEA

The overall trends outlined in the preceding chapter are amply reinforced and elucidated by data from other sources. As a nation we are not only rapidly growing in population but also developing land twice as rapidly as the pace of population growth nationally, much faster in some places. Moreover, according to the Natural Resources Inventory of the U.S. Department of Agriculture, the already rapid pace of land development has been accelerating, from 1.4 million acres per year in the 1980s to 2.1 million per year in the 1990s. The Department of Agriculture data disclose that 30 percent of all developed land in the U.S. was developed in just 19 recent years, from 1982 to 2001.

Population and land-use trends also reveal a number of important regional distinctions. In the past two decades, the West has been growing and sprawling but not sprawling quite as much as the national average; the Northeast and the Midwest have been sprawling but not growing much; and the South continues both to grow and to sprawl rapidly. These trends are summarized in Figure 3-1, derived from a recent study sponsored by the Brookings Institution.

The cumulative impact of all this dispersal is that, as of the 2000 census, suburbs held over 60 percent of the U.S. metropolitan population.

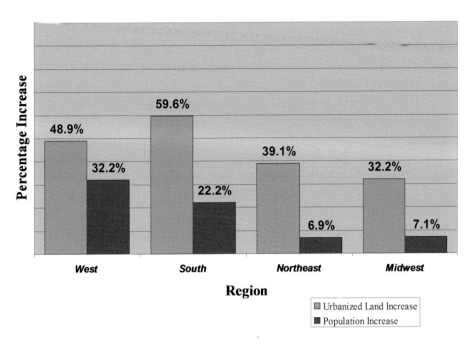

Fig. 3-1: Population versus urbanized land growth by region, 1982–1997, as summarized in Who Sprawls Most? How Growth Patterns Differ Across the U.S., *prepared in July 2001 by William Fulton, et al. for the Brookings Institution's Center for Urban and Metropolitan Policy.*

The average population density of all developed areas in 1920 was a little less than 10 persons per acre; by 2000, the average had declined to only 3.75 people per acre. Under current trends, the decline will continue, since about four-fifths of the country's growth in the coming decades is expected to locate in suburbs and other fringe locations that collectively spread development beyond the current outer reaches of our metro areas. Partly as a result, the Maryland Office of Planning has projected that, from 1995 to 2020, more land will be converted to housing in the Chesapeake Bay region than in the past three and one-half centuries.[2]

Workplace trends are just as dramatic, if not more so. The hundreds of "edge cities" consisting of offices and shopping, located along freeways on the suburban fringe of our metropolitan areas, contained some two-thirds of all U.S. office space as of the mid-1990s, and the share has undoubtedly grown since then. Henry Diamond and Patrick Noonan reported in their 1996 book, *Land Use in America,* that an astonishing 95 percent of the new office jobs created in the latter part of the twentieth century were located in low-density suburbs.[3] This reflects major job growth on the fringe; suburbs of all types held only 25 percent of the country's office space as recently as 1970. However, some suburban job "growth" can be illusory when placed in a broader context; in fact, many "new" jobs are really only jobs displaced from other locations.

The pervasiveness of contemporary job dispersal is illustrated plainly in Los Angeles, where in the 1990s the 19 largest geographic job centers, even taken together and including Los Angeles's downtown, held only 17 to 18 percent of the region's jobs.[4] Four of the six counties in the nation that added the most jobs in 2003 and 2004 are in Southern California: Orange County, south of Los Angeles (tops in the country, adding 49,900 jobs); Los Angeles County; and Riverside and San Bernardino counties, east of Los Angeles.[5]

For both residential and commercial development, the predominant pattern of recent growth has taken a strikingly different form from what our country has experienced throughout most of its history. Although American settlements have been growing and evolving since colonial times, until the middle of the twentieth century we tended to locate in recognizable cities and towns. Our changes were much more gradual and reflective of customary patterns of town layout and structure, with little significant departure from longstanding principles of lot size and street geometry. Today, despite the desire for strong local communities voiced by many Americans, the result is likely to be much more chaotic. Joel Garreau, the author of the 1991 book, *Edge City: Life on the New Frontier*, describes a typical edge city in New Jersey called "287 and 78" (named for the intersection of two Interstate highways). There are no political boundaries in 287 and 78, no elected ruling structure, and no overall leader; instead, it is "governed" only by a patchwork of generally uncoordinated and conflicting zoning, planning, and county boards.[6]

The diverse array of forms that dispersed land development takes, along with its geographic elusiveness, makes it hard to measure. But the nonprofit coalition Smart Growth America has recently undertaken a study that compares regions on a number of indicators related to density, mix of land uses, intra-regional connectedness, and centeredness. The study found that the 10 "most sprawling" metropolitan areas in the U.S. are all squarely within the multi-city regions described in the preceding chapter: Riverside-San Bernardino and Oxnard-Ventura near Los Angeles in California; Atlanta and four other metropolitan regions in the Southeast; Fort. Worth-Arlington, Texas; Bridgeport-Stamford-Norwalk-Danbury, Connecticut; and West Palm Beach-Boca Raton-Delray Beach, Florida.[7]

BIG, BIGGER, BIGGEST

As impressive as the data concerning population and job dispersal may be, they mask another way that we are spreading out as we grow: We are constructing ever-larger buildings. In 1970, the average new single-family house contained 1,400 square feet; today it's 2,300, although household size has been declining steadily. In 1950, each American claimed an average of 312 square feet of living space; by 1993, the amount had more than doubled, to 742 square feet. This is 50 to 100 percent more than the space occupied by the average residents of over 50 nations surveyed by the World Bank in the 1990s.[8]

Moreover, the size of some new commercial buildings would astound our grandparents. The Bishop Ranch development, 30 miles east of San Francisco, contains a "landscraper" three stories high and over half a mile long. The building that houses Ameritech's headquarters, west of O'Hare International Airport near Chicago, is also more than half a mile long. And cars can claim more space in such developments than people: A typical suburban office park might provide 1,400 square feet of parking, usually in surface lots, for every 1,000 square feet of floor space.

Further, the amount of total retail space per American doubled from 1960 to 1998.[9] A new Wal-Mart "supercenter" can claim 200,000 square feet of indoor space, much larger than the 120,000 square feet occupied by the typical Wal-Mart of just 10 years ago, and a staggering 30 times bigger than a typical Dollar General Store. Including its parking lot, a new Wal-Mart can occupy over 20 acres of land. These big-box stores, power centers, and the like represented more than 80 percent of all new shopping built in the 1990s.[10]

The new stores shape the landscape not only when they are thriving but perhaps even more so when they are abandoned, decaying eyesores in communities left behind by investment flight to ever-newer areas. The problem is compounded by the changing nature of retailing in America, as continued growth in the share of mail order and Internet sales threatens further inroads into superstores' on-site business. Some analysts have predicted that as many as 20 percent of today's suburban shopping centers could be dead or dying within a decade.

RUNAROUND SUE

There are a host of troubling consequences that attach to our current patterns of growth, many of them related to the increased automobile dependence that is associated with sprawl. As we spread ourselves farther and farther apart, it becomes inevitable that we must travel longer distances to work, shop, enjoy recreation, and visit family and friends. The convenience store and even the playground may no longer be within walking distance. Work may be on the other side of town or in another town altogether. The bus stop may be farther away, too, even if we are fortunate enough to have a bus that goes anywhere close to our destination; in many places, there is no bus service at all.

The only good choice for most suburbanites is to drive, and to drive a lot. And that is exactly what we are doing. Motor vehicle miles traveled in the U.S. have been on an upward trend for several decades. According to the federal Bureau of Transportation Statistics, vehicle use in the U.S. doubled from one to just over two trillion miles per year between 1970 and 1990, and had climbed to over 2.8 trillion miles by 2002. Although growth in annual vehicle miles traveled slowed somewhat in the 1990s to around two percent per year, down from the three- and four-percent annual growth rates experienced in the 1980s, the numbers continue to go up. The rate grew 2.7 percent from 2001 to 2002, the last year for which incremental data are available.[11]

A number of troubling additional trends are associated with the growth of vehicle use in recent decades, all pointing to increased inefficiency in travel patterns. These include an increase in average trip length, growth in the number of vehicle trips taken per person and per household per year, a decline in all modes of travel other than single-occupancy driving, and a decline in average vehicle occupancy. [Figure 3-2]

While there are a number of possible reasons for the growth in automobile travel, there is little question that land development patterns are a major part of the cause. Environmental researcher John Holtzclaw has been studying the relationships between vehicle use and neighborhood densities in a number of metropolitan regions, including San Francisco, Los Angeles, and Chicago, for a decade. Holtzclaw's work shows that vehicle use increases as neighborhoods become more spread out and, conversely, that use declines as neighborhoods become more compact and more typically urban. His analysis of travel data in a number of studies and communities indicates that, as residential density doubles,

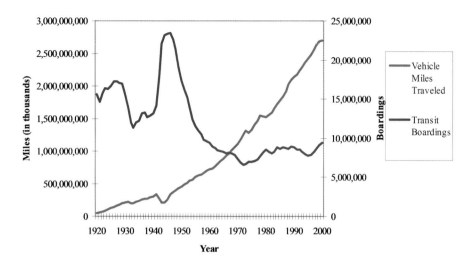

Fig. 3-2: Change in Transit Boardings and Vehicle Miles Traveled 1920–2000. Data originally from USDOT, American Public Transit Association, as provided by the Surface Transportation Policy Project.

vehicle use declines some 20 to 40 percent. Vehicle trips per household, as well as vehicle mileage driven, decline with each incremental increase in density, and the basic conclusions hold true even when the analysis is controlled for such variables as household size and income. Other research has been generally consistent with the comprehensive work done by Holtzclaw.[12]

While spread-out development generates substantially more automobile and truck traffic than compact communities do, this seems especially true when low-density development is coupled with other neighborhood characteristics. These include the isolation of community functions—housing, work, shopping, recreation, education—in single-use tracts, a lack of pedestrian amenities, and neighborhood location that fails to coordinate well with the rest of a metropolitan region. Unfortunately, we are not only sprawling out; we are doing so in a way that guarantees increased automobile dependence.

STUCK IN THE MIDDLE WITH YOU

It will come as no surprise to soccer moms and dads, delivery drivers, and suburban commuters that all this increased driving has substantially increased traffic congestion: Americans now spend roughly one of every eight waking hours in their cars. Seventy percent of peak-hour travel on urban interstate highways now occurs on congested roads operating at more than 80 percent capacity. Average time of congestion daily on metropolitan roadways essentially doubled from two to three hours in 1982 to five to six hours by 1999. The Surface Transportation Policy Project, observing that American women, especially mothers, have become "the bus drivers of the 1990s," reports that women now drive an average of 29 miles per day, spending more time in their cars than the average American spends in conversation.[13]

According to the annual study of urban mobility and traffic congestion published by the Texas Transportation Institute, the impacts on drivers in the fast-spreading multi-city regions described in this book are substantial indeed. Drivers in Los Angeles endure an average of 93 hours per year in congestion-related delays; Orlando drivers lose 51 hours, and Atlanta drivers lose 60 hours. Average annual delays in Dallas have increased more than fourfold, from 13 hours in 1982 to 61 hours in 2002. The institute has concluded that congestion cost the American economy some $63 billion in lost productivity and wasted fuel in 2004.

Even when traffic congestion is viewed in isolation from related transportation impacts, there is no quick fix. For the latter half of the twentieth century, American planners, engineers, and decision makers relied mostly on the expansion of road system capacity to alleviate traffic congestion. As quoted in *Divided Highways*, historian Tom Lewis's chronicle of the U.S. interstate highway system, even back in June 1969 President Nixon's Transportation Secretary, John Volpe, lamented that "[t]he federal government spends as much money on highway construction in six weeks as it has put into urban transit in the last six years. . . . Unless we intend to pave the entire surface of the country—and no one wants that—we have to stop this trend. We already have one mile of highway for every square mile of land area in the U.S.A."[14] A little over three decades later, we now have two lane miles for every square mile of land.

Even if we wanted to, we could not afford to build enough additional highway lane miles to keep pace with our burgeoning population and expansive land development. But, even if we could, it wouldn't work. This is because new road capacity acts as a powerful magnet for drivers, inducing us to take more and longer trips than we otherwise would take, soon congesting the very roads we built to alleviate congestion. According to the growing academic literature on "induced travel," as summarized in a 2000 presentation by Lewison Lee Lem of the U.S. Environmental Protection Agency, every 10 percent increase in road capacity leads to two to five percent more driving in the short term and five to 10 percent increases in the long term, essentially putting affected regions right back where they started.

Some of this additional traffic appears because the new road capacity also induces more land development. A recent study performed for the Brookings Institution by Marlon Boarnet found that highway investments shift economic development away from existing communities to newly built areas. Just as empty roads and traffic lanes act as magnets for new driving, highway interchanges draw new development.

RUNNING ON EMPTY

These dramatic increases in motor vehicle travel cause a host of serious environmental problems, including increases in energy consumption, greenhouse gas emissions, and unhealthful air pollution. Transportation is by far the largest consumer of petroleum products in the U.S., accounting for two-thirds of our overall oil consumption. Transportation alone consumes more oil than the nation produces, and more oil than we import, each year. The Bureau of Transportation Statistics reports that, as of 2001, the U.S. was using around 13 million barrels of oil each day to support our transportation habits, up from 9.55 million in 1980. That is a 38 percent increase in only two decades. Slightly more than half of U.S. transportation energy is consumed by cars, SUVs, and other personal vehicles, with heavier freight trucks accounting for around a fourth. Gasoline consumption in the U.S. alone accounts for 11 percent of world oil consumption. [Figure 3-3, page 26]

Our gluttonous appetite for oil is uniquely American, at least as a matter of degree. Long-term research on 48 cities around the world by Australian professors Peter Newman and Jeffrey Kenworthy indicates that, on average, residents of the U.S. consume four times as much gasoline per capita as do residents of Europe, and nine times as much as residents of Asian cities. [Figure 3-4, page 26]

Even after correcting for economic factors such as income levels, gasoline prices, and fuel efficiencies, the authors have found that gasoline consumption and automobile usage is still significantly higher in the U.S. than in other parts of the world, on average. Automobile use per capita in the U.S. is 2.41 times that in Europe despite economic productivity per capita being only 0.85 that of Europe.[15]

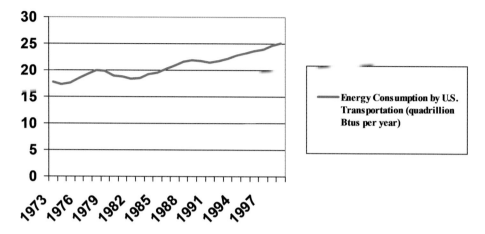

Fig. 3-3: Increase in Energy Consumption by U.S. Transportation Sector, Data from U.S. Department of Energy.

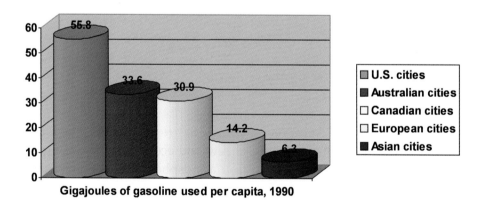

Fig. 3-4: Gasoline use per capita in the U.S., Canada, Europe, Australia and Asia, from Newman and Kenworthy: Sustainability and Cities.

This creates immense pressure to open up rich and pristine natural areas such as the Arctic National Wildlife Refuge and waters off the California coast to oil exploration, and it contributes to international political anxiety. In a speech in Washington in October 2004, former Federal Reserve chairman Alan Greenspan gave expression to some of the concerns:

> [T]he current situation reflects an increasing fear that existing reserves and productive crude oil capacity have become subject to potential geopolitical adversity. These anxieties patently are not frivolous given the stark realities evident in many areas of the world . . . . [G]rowing uncertainties about the long-term security of world oil production, especially in the Middle East, have been pressing oil prices sharply higher. . . .[16]

Greenspan went on to note that much of the capital infrastructure of the U.S. and elsewhere was built in anticipation of lower real oil prices than currently prevail or are anticipated for the future, and that the situation will only be subject to additional pressures as China and India continue to industrialize and increase their oil consumption. As oil and gasoline prices rise, the oil- and gasoline-intensive economy of the U.S. will only become increasingly burdened compared to those countries with more energy-efficient economies, and our patterns of land development, unless reversed, will make those burdens very difficult to address.

One inevitable by-product of all the fossil fuel consumption brought on by increasing automobile dependence is the emission of carbon dioxide, a potent greenhouse gas. According to data from the federal Departments of Transportation and Energy, transportation in the U.S. produces over 450 million metric tons of carbon dioxide each year, about a third of all U.S. carbon emissions. Total U.S. carbon emissions have been growing at an average rate of about one percent per year, with transportation sources growing around 20 percent faster than the total. Carbon emissions per capita in the U.S. are nearly double those in Europe.

So far, the effects on our quality of life and economy from rising accumulation of greenhouse gases in our atmosphere have not been dramatic. But they could become so. While it is beyond the scope of this chapter to document the likely patterns and consequences of global warming, the Intergovernmental Panel on Climate Change has developed a range of projections of future climate trends, all of them indicating that average rates of warming probably will be greater than any seen in the last 10,000 years. The IPCC's mid-range, "best estimate" forecast is for an additional 2° Centigrade (3.6° Fahrenheit) warming in the twenty-first century. The "best estimate" scenario also forecasts an additional sea level rise of about 50 centimeters (20 inches) during the same time period.[17]

The resulting impacts on human health and ecosystems could be widespread and quite serious, ranging from sea level rise and flooding to widespread transmission of vector-borne diseases. While the American responses to calls from the international community of nations to contain greenhouse gas emissions have been anything but clear or strong, under any scenario it will be difficult to address the issues if emissions from the our country's transportation sector continue to rise so dramatically.

EVERY BREATH YOU TAKE

The news on unhealthful air pollution from our sprawling driving patterns is only slightly more encouraging. A report from the federal Environmental Protection Agency summarizes the situation:

> Despite considerable progress, the overall goal of clean and healthy air continues to elude much of the country. Unhealthy air pollution levels still plague virtually every major city in the United States. This is largely because development and urban sprawl have created new pollution sources and have contributed to a doubling of vehicle travel since 1970.[18]

That is even clearer today than in 1994, when the report was written. Cars and other highway vehicles continue to emit some 60 million tons of carbon monoxide per year, about 62 percent of our national inventory of that pollutant; cars and other highway vehicles continue to emit some seven million tons per year, almost 27 percent of our volatile organic compounds (VOCs), which constitute a major precursor to ozone smog; and they emit around eight million tons per year, about 37 percent of our nitrogen oxides, another ozone precursor.[19] Motor vehicles also emit as much as half of our carcinogenic and toxic air pollutants, such as benzene and formaldehyde. And heavy vehicles, particularly diesel-powered buses and freight trucks, constitute a significant source of soot and other unhealthful fine particles.

The transportation sector is responsible for more than half of the total emissions of federally regulated pollutants in a number of regions found among this book's multi-city regions. According to 1999 data reported by the Surface Transportation Policy Project, regions whose emissions are predominantly from transportation include the following: Fort

Worth-Arlington (transportation responsible for 60.2 percent), San Antonio (57.1 percent), Los Angeles-Long Beach (56.9 percent), Austin-San Marcos (56.9 percent), Dallas (56.7 percent), Hartford (55.6 percent), New York (53.9 percent), Seattle-Bellevue-Everett (53.6 percent), Detroit (52.7 percent), and Raleigh-Durham-Chapel Hill (50.5 percent).[20]

EPA scientists believe that current trends in vehicle trips and miles driven, even with continuing incremental improvements in emission control systems, threaten to reverse the recent national trend of improving air quality by causing total emissions of carbon dioxide, sulfur dioxide, and particulate matter to increase in the near future.[21] Total nitrogen oxide emissions from motor vehicles already are at a higher level than they were two decades ago.[22] As a result, the steady improvement nationally in ozone smog levels that had been experienced before the mid-1990s has essentially come to a halt, with smog no longer decreasing in most metropolitan areas. In 2002, Los Angeles experienced over 100 days with unhealthy air quality, as measured by the federal EPA. And Austin, Boston, Charlotte, Greensboro, and Orlando are among the cities that experienced over 50 percent increases in the number of unhealthy smog levels at the turn of the twenty-first century, compared with those experienced in the mid-1990s.[23] Because smog levels tend to increase with hotter summers, current warming trends will only exacerbate the situation.

These numbers matter to our quality of life and our economy. Air pollution from tailpipe emissions is linked with a range of pulmonary, coronary, and neurological diseases, including asthma, cancer, heart disease, heart attacks, strokes, high blood pressure, birth defects, and brain damage. Asthma, in particular, has increased sharply in the last decade. Transportation-related public health costs from air pollution were estimated to be more than $1.5 billion in New York and Los Angeles, respectively, in 2001. The costs were high in other metro areas as well, approximately $1 billion in Chicago and $500 million to $600 million each in Atlanta, Dallas-Fort Worth, Detroit, Houston, Philadelphia, San Francisco-Oakland and Washington, D.C.[24] And beyond its human health impacts, air pollution also is detrimental to ecosystem health, contributing to such recognized threats as acid rain and excess nitrogen loading to aquatic and terrestrial systems.

Sprawl-related automobile dependence is also becoming known as one of the factors contributing to a decline in walking and associated physical activity in our daily life, complicating efforts to address alarming rates of obesity and hypertension in America. Nearly 63 percent of Americans are overweight, and nearly one in three is now classified as obese. The association of sprawling neighborhoods with expanding waistlines has now been documented by researchers at, among other places, Harvard and Emory universities, the Centers for Disease Control, and Smart Growth America, whose 2003 comprehensive study of the available data indicates that those of us who live in the most sprawling areas are likely to walk 25 to 30 percent less than those of us in the least sprawling areas, and are likely to weigh some six pounds more.

An ongoing study in Atlanta is finding that, as housing density increases from two units per acre to eight units per acre, the proportion of white men who are overweight drops from 68 percent to 50 percent and the proportion of obese men drops from 23 to 13 percent. These findings are holding true for other sectors of the population as well. Physical inactivity leads to over 200,000 premature deaths per year, and research shows that people who walk regularly have half the number of sick days for colds and other respiratory infections that are suffered by those who do not.[25]

ONCE THERE WERE GREENFIELDS

Beyond the impacts related to traffic and mobility, sprawling land development is dramatically altering the character of our nation's landscape and the resources it harbors. We can literally see the impacts to our working farms and our ecosystems, and to the once-familiar vistas that for generations have soothed our spirit and nourished our ever-more-tenuous connection as human beings to the mysteries of the natural world.

While the U.S. continues to enjoy the appearance of abundant farmland, the best of that land is being lost permanently to development. Drawing from its research on the subject, the American Farmland Trust concluded in its report *Farming on the Edge* that the nation's inventory of cropland declined 12 percent in just two recent decades, from 420 million acres in 1982 to 368 million acres in 2002. The rate of conversion to non-farm uses accelerated in the last decade, with land used for farming and ranching declining 51 percent faster in the 1990s than in the 1980s. Several states saw the rate of their farmland loss more than double during the years from 1992 to 1997 compared to the five previous years. They include Illinois, New York, New Jersey, Maryland, and Connecticut, all of which serve the multi-city regions highlighted in this book. In those five years, the nation as a whole lost six million acres of farmland, an area the size of Maryland.[26]

To make matters worse, most of the country's prime farmland, the land with soil and climatic conditions best suited for growing crops, is located within the fast-expanding suburban and exurban counties of metropolitan areas. Such "urban-influenced" counties currently produce more than half the total value of U.S. farm production; counties with prime and unique farmland found by the Farmland Trust to be threatened by particularly high rates of current development collectively produce some 86 percent of our nation's fruits and vegetables.

Poorly planned development also creates fragmented ecosystems that can no longer support the most imperiled wildlife species, which require large, undisturbed areas. So-called "leapfrog" or scattered development leaves only smaller, more isolated patches suited mainly for generalist species that are already abundant. These effects are cumulative and worsen over time so that, although the U.S. has enjoyed success through the federal Endangered Species Act and other efforts at meeting the needs of high-profile species in certain locations, we are witnessing a slow decline of others, especially songbirds and amphibians.

There is ample reason to take better care of our ecological resources. Research done for the Biological Resources Division of the U.S. Geological Survey reports that 27 ecosystem types have declined by 98 percent or more since the European settlement of North America. More than 500 species of plants and animals have become extinct in America since that time, and over twice that many are currently listed by the U.S. Fish and Wildlife Service as threatened or endangered. The Nature Conservancy, in a comprehensive assessment of some 20,000 species of plants and animals native to the U.S., reports that current extinction rates are conservatively estimated to be at least 10,000 times greater than naturally occurring levels, largely because of habitat degradation and destruction.

The loss of biologically rich wetlands is of particular concern. According to the Fish and Wildlife Service, the U.S. has lost some 117 million acres of wetlands, more than half the original base, since the first European settlement, and continues to lose 58,000 acres per year. The leading causes are urban and rural development, together accounting for 51 percent of the loss, outpacing agriculture (26 percent) and silviculture (23 percent).[27]

Ecosystem losses have been especially pronounced in some fast-growing areas of the country. California is estimated to have lost over

90 percent of its original wetland resource. That state is also estimated to have lost over 90 percent of its native grassland, over 80 percent of its coastal redwoods, and over 70 percent of its coastal sage. The National Wildlife Federation identifies low-density development as the leading cause of overall species imperilment in California, contributing to the imperilment of 188 of the 286 California species listed as threatened or endangered under the Endangered Species Act.

Six other states—Illinois, Indiana, Iowa, Kentucky, Missouri, and Ohio—have also lost more than 80 percent of their original wetlands. Dryland habitat is under siege, too: In fast-developing Florida, 15 of the state's upland-community ecosystem types are said to be imperiled, some critically; Florida has lost over 80 percent of its longleaf and slash pine forests. In Pennsylvania, the Pocono till barrens and serpentine barrens, which hold that state's two largest concentrations of land-based endangered species, are now under severe threat because they are being opened to suburban development.[28]

Haphazard, low-density development also wreaks havoc on our nation's water quality. Natural landscapes, such as forests, wetlands, and grasslands, are typically varied and porous. They trap rainwater and snowmelt and filter it into the ground slowly. When there is runoff, it tends to reach receiving waterways gradually. Developed areas, in contrast, are characterized by large paved or covered surfaces (think of a supermarket parking lot leading to a connecting road and to a freeway) that are impervious to rain. Instead of percolating slowly into the ground, storm water becomes trapped above these surfaces, accumulates, and runs off in large amounts into streams, lakes, and estuaries, picking up pollutants along the way. Along with increased water volume come changes in composition as contaminants, including sediment, pathogens, nutrients (such as nitrogen and phosphorous), heavy metals, pesticides, and nondegradable debris, are picked up. As a result, there is a strong correlation between the amount of imperviousness in a drainage basin and the health of its receiving stream.

Pavement and associated runoff pollution affect more and more watersheds. On-site measures to assist water quality, such as maximizing natural ground cover in individual lots, are overwhelmed by the larger system of roadways and parking lots required to serve certain types of development. Research shows that large-lot subdivisions increase imperviousness by 10 to 50 percent compared to cluster and traditional town developments with the same number of households, and that they deliver up to three times more sediment into waterways.

The consequences of watershed degradation from development have been felt across the country, nowhere more dramatically than in the Gulf Coast regions savaged by Hurricanes Katrina and Rita in the fall of 2005. While wetlands and coastal barrier islands provide natural buffers against flooding, more than 1,900 square miles of Louisiana's wetlands have disappeared since 1930, much of that due to development. Wetland losses continue at a rate of 24 square miles per year, according to conservation organizations.[29] As a result, New Orleans and nearby coastal communities had little natural resistance to the flood waters that eventually overwhelmed levees and caused the most extensive storm damage in our nation's history. Similarly, in the Puget Sound region of Washington State, major floods that were 25-year events now occur annually. "The sponge is full," according to King County analyst Tom Kiney. In Akron, Ohio, runoff from residential areas has been estimated at up to 10 times that of pre-development conditions, and runoff from commercial development has been estimated at 18 times that before development.[30] In several Maryland, Pennsylvania, and Virginia watersheds that drain into the Chesapeake Bay, pollution from development has been found to exceed—in some cases dramatically—pollution from industry and agriculture. Even in counties that have enacted stormwater-management regulations, the pace of development is causing pollutant loads to increase.

BROTHER, CAN YOU SPARE A DIME?

In addition to the environmental ramifications of sprawling land use, the economic impacts—and their potentially troubling implications for the sustainability of American competitiveness in the coming decades—are profound. The drain on the American economy is manifested in a number of ways, from strained municipal and household budgets to reduced worker productivity.

Regarding the former, there is no question that fiscal stress has been brewing in our cities and towns, in fast-growing jurisdictions on the fringe of metropolitan areas and in center cities alike. Every day, public officials and newspaper articles recount stories of the need to trim municipal budgets, cut services, and raise additional revenue. And our inefficient and costly growth patterns contribute substantially to the fiscal stress. As it was put in a 1998 Environmental Protection Agency report, "Many of America's local governments are in the grip of a growing fiscal crisis. . . . Although the details of the story differ, they are linked by one recurring theme: much of the fiscal crisis stems from growth and development that could no longer be sustained."[31]

As we build homes, workplaces, and shops, we must find or build a network of infrastructure to service them. In addition to the driveways and utility lines that are needed on each building site, there are a number of categories that are typically furnished by the community at large, frequently at public cost. These include neighborhood costs such as collector streets, water distribution lines, sewer collector lines, and recreational facilities; community costs such as roads, water and sewer trunk lines, electricity lines, telephone lines, schools, emergency services (police, fire, and rescue), libraries, and parks; and regional costs such as regional roads, central water and sewer treatment, solid waste disposal, and central electricity and telephone facilities. Sprawl development costs more across all categories because it requires more infrastructure and more travel for service per unit.

But the cost of building new infrastructure is only the beginning. The fiscal strain imposed by growth may only get worse for many jurisdictions because of the high costs of operation and maintenance. Across the country, we have focused our resources for the last half-century (and, because of our development patterns, continue to focus them) on constructing a vast network of roads, sewers, schools, power lines, and other facilities necessary to accommodate growth without sufficiently preparing for the time when that network would need to be repaired or replaced. As this infrastructure inevitably ages and deteriorates, we must now pay in increasing amounts for maintaining it.

Planners for the Los Angeles region concluded in the 1990s that $37 billion would be needed just for operation and maintenance of the area's road network between 1996 and 2020.[32] That is more than $2,000 for every individual in the region, reducing funds available for new and better transportation facilities. Similarly, in Kansas City, where in the mid-1990s there were more freeway miles per person than in any other major metropolitan area in the country, the Chamber of Commerce estimated that repairing neglected infrastructure would cost more than $2 billion. This is more than $1,250 for each person in the metropolitan area.[33]

The costs of growth-related infrastructure are sometimes exposed as especially wasteful when viewed in the context of a region as a whole.

This is because, as metropolitan areas expand, "new" suburban growth is not always new; substantial portions of it may instead just be displaced from other parts of the metropolitan area. In Montgomery County, Maryland, although the countywide school population *dropped* by 10,000 pupils between 1980 and 1990, 70 new schools were built and 68 others were abandoned.[34] This has a damaging effect on a region's economy in both old and new locations: Cities and inner suburbs must repair and replace aging infrastructure with fewer taxpayers to cover the costs, while newer suburbs must find the resources to pay for costly new infrastructure to support growth. The result of displaced growth is a "lose-lose" combination for both types of jurisdictions.

The problem is particularly acute in many communities because sprawling developments rarely generate enough new revenues from taxes and traditional fees to cover the costs of providing infrastructure and services. Impact fees, where they are imposed, help to some degree, but not enough. In the end, new growth is subsidized by a variety of sources, including taxpayers and other users of public services infrastructure, in the form of increased taxes and user fees.

Many jurisdictions respond by trying to attract commercial development—sometimes with aggressive tax benefits—to generate positive revenues. Such development, which is thought to require no school construction and a reduced amount of police, fire, and other public services, is widely believed to be a revenue winner. But, in fact, commercial development often creates a demand for additional nearby residential development, bringing a fiscal drain that offsets the benefits. In response, local governments may seek to attract still more commercial development to offset the costs of providing public services to the just-attracted residential developments. The result is a vicious cycle in which many jurisdictions are constantly failing in their attempt to pay for residential growth with nonresidential development.[35]

At the national level, the voluminous study *Costs of Sprawl-2000,* by Rutgers University's Robert Burchell and associates, projects that current development trends will cost 25 percent more in public funds over 25 years than would a planned growth scenario that concentrated new development in and around existing communities. A business-as-usual approach would require, among other things, 188,300 more new lane-miles of road capacity at a cost of $110 billion, and 4.6 million more miles of additional water and sewer lines at a cost of $12.6 billion over the time period.[36]

Households also feel the effects of low-density development. With the increased automobile dependence and longer trips required by spread-out development, Americans now spend more on transportation than on food, clothing, or health care. According to the U.S. Department of Labor, as of 2001, 19.3 cents from every household dollar are spent on transportation, which is a close second only to housing in its claim on earnings. The share has grown from 14 cents in 1960 and from under 10 cents in 1935.

Transportation expenses are an even greater burden for poorer families. According to the Surface Transportation Policy Project, the poorest 20 percent of American families spend 40 percent of their take-home pay on transportation, and the working poor spend nearly 10 percent of their income just getting to work. Those who drive to work spend 21 percent of their income commuting. The actual burden may now be even greater for both poor and average households, given that these calculations were based on data collected before the steady and steep increase in gasoline prices suffered by American consumers beginning in 2002. Chicago's Center for Neighborhood Technology, which has spent over a decade researching the relationship between transportation costs and housing, has found that families that must spend a large share of their income on purchasing, operating, and maintaining cars and trucks often cannot save enough to own a home.

Places with more compact development patterns and more robust public transit systems can be kinder to household budgets. Newman and Kenworthy, the Australian researchers who study international transportation patterns, report that households in European and Asian cities spend only eight percent and five percent, respectively, of their incomes on transportation, despite higher fuel costs. Looking at U.S. metropolitan areas, the Surface Transportation Policy Project found that households in the most sprawling areas spend substantially more on transportation than households in the least sprawling areas. In 1997 and 1998, households devoted the highest portion of their budget to transportation in spread-out Houston, Atlanta, Dallas-Fort Worth, Miami, and Detroit. The average Houston area household spent 22 cents out of every dollar on transportation, spending well over $8,800 each year to get around, or $2,528 more than the national average. The three least expensive (and, not coincidentally, among the most dense) metro areas in the survey, New York, Baltimore, and Honolulu, spent almost one-third less: Baltimore households used less than 15 cents out of every dollar on transportation, spending $5,236 annually. That amount translates to a savings of over $3,000 per year compared to Houston.[37]

The European and Asian economies also benefit from lower rates of road accidents, which cost the U.S. some $150 billion each year. Newman and Kenworthy report that European metro regions experience 8.8 traffic fatalities annually per 100,000 people, as compared with 14.6 fatalities per year in this country.

There is also an emerging body of evidence showing that low-density land development can degrade general economic efficiency and productivity. To the extent this is true, the implications for American competitiveness in a global economy are obvious. In an extensive review of the literature on the fiscal and competitive impacts of development patterns, researchers Mark Muro and Robert Puentes found for the Brookings Institution that the relationship can be seen from a variety of different measures with consistent conclusions.[38]

Research on communities within the greater San Francisco region has found that spread-out areas fared worse on a number of economic performance indicators than did more compactly developed areas. At the state level, workers in the 10 states with the most spread-out populations produced 25 percent less economic value than workers in the 10 states with the densest populations. Areas that are more spread-out also produce fewer patents, which tend to rise 20 to 30 percent on average as population density doubles.

This undoubtedly is due in part to the costs of congestion, travel distance, and other transportation inefficiencies built into the distribution of goods and services needed for American business and its consumers. In their publication *Smart Growth Is Smart Business*, the National Association of Local Environmental Professionals and the Smart Growth Leadership Institute observed that the lack of nearby affordable housing in Howard County, Maryland, means that businesses must fund shuttle buses to pick up workers in Baltimore and bring them to suburban malls 20 miles from the city. As noted, the effects of these inefficiencies are likely to worsen as oil and gasoline costs rise. The same report also noted the costs of lost productivity due to traffic congestion and worker absenteeism in automobile-dependent communities.

Newman and Kenworthy observe that the U.S. spends 24 percent more of its gross economic product on trips to work than does Europe, which is more compactly developed, and that Europe has a higher rate of economic output per capita than does the U.S.: almost $5,000 per person per year. European business is stronger than ever: Europe leads the world in a number of industries from aerospace to insurance, and 14 of the 20 largest commercial banks in the world are European. Sixty-one of the 140 biggest companies on the global Fortune 500 list are European, as compared with 50 American companies. There are also more poor people in the U.S. than in the combined 16 European countries for which data are available.[39] While the inefficiencies associated with land development patterns may be but one factor among many behind these trends, the implications should be sobering for American business.

LIVING JUST ENOUGH FOR THE CITY

All these serious problems aside, some of the most severe and troubling consequences of the way we are growing are those felt by populations left behind. The migration of residents, jobs, and economic investment to America's sprawling outer suburbs has been devastating to many inner-city neighborhoods, including a disproportionate number of minority communities. The draining of wealth, resources, and spirit from these neighborhoods has meant that many of those who have remained have become isolated from mainstream society, making it increasingly difficult for them to access jobs, educational opportunities, medical services, and other prerequisites of the American Dream. In 1960, central cities contained one-third of the nation's poor; by 1990, the central-city share had climbed to one-half, even though the central-city share of total population had declined to around 30 percent.

In many locations, the wave of suburbanization and road-building that characterized the last half-century (and continues today) destroyed communities in a quite literal way. Some 335,000 housing units, mainly in inner cities, were razed during the first decade of interstate highway construction. In Nashville, the construction of I-40 went straight through 80 percent of the city's African American businesses, while also demolishing 650 homes and 27 apartment buildings and creating a physical barrier separating its largest African American universities from each other and from important parts of their community.[40]

The long-term effect of the transfer of economic activity and affluence to increasingly distant suburban locations has been a diminished tax base and a sustained cycle of decline in many older communities. The decline in the quality of amenities and services caused by a diminished tax base affects the communities' ability to attract new residents and jobs, which only further diminishes the tax base and fiscal capacity to address the problems.

Smaller towns, too, experience abandonment and disinvestment. Local "mom-and-pop" businesses have been undermined by the explosion of discount retailing that accompanies low-density development: the superstores, commercial strips, and malls located along major roadways that take advantage of cheap land, cheap energy, cheap labor, and generous local tax breaks and incentives. A 1996 article in the *Kansas City Star* discussed the ways in which Interstate 70 dramatically changed the character of small towns after malls and discount outlets sprang up along its route. One long-time resident explained that "[the highway] killed our old downtown," arguing that it lost grocery stores, a cobbler, the bank, and other businesses because of competition from these superstores.[41]

Problems once regarded as "urban" have reached the suburbs, which are now experiencing their own cycle of decline and abandonment. In his book *Metropolitics*, Myron Orfield presents maps showing how living conditions have changed over time within sprawling metropolitan areas. In addition to showing the simple geographic progression of land development, the maps graphically document the spread of problems such as unemployment, poor educational performance, and crime from central city neighborhoods to inner-ring suburbs. With regard to Chicago, Orfield notes that in the 1990s, nine suburbs had higher crime rates than that of Chicago proper, and 40 had rates above the regional average. In their analysis of the literature on fiscal and economic effects, Muro and Puentes observed that the impacts are felt well beyond those neighborhoods where they are obvious: "Urban decay can undercut the attractiveness of the entire region by harming its ability to maintain the physical infrastructure, reducing the number of regionally valued amenities, weakening its agglomeration economies, and imposing other social costs manifested by high crime, poor health, and unproductive workers."[42]

Even in crime-free, affluent suburbs—those to which the investment has fled—quality of life can suffer. The most common observation is that the design—and frequent chaos—of low-density development discourages interaction among residents and forces people to go outside their communities even for the most basic shopping errands, social visits, and work. All too frequently, as Don Chen, executive director of Smart Growth America, has written, "residents tend to interact with their neighbors mainly through their windshields"—not the most social form of human interaction.[43] And the additional time spent driving eats directly into leisure and professional time.

It does not help that many "edge cities" and other new, outer suburbs exhibit a striking lack of political or cultural coherence, with relatively few civic and cultural institutions to provide any sort of unifying force. Cul-de-sac street design also prevents individual developments from connecting with each other and, in some cases, walls and gates are erected for the very purpose of isolating developments from the outside world. The relative absence of pedestrian activity is often identified as a particular threat to community cohesion because walking is conducive to chance encounters and the creation of informal relationships within communities. In much of new suburbia, non-drivers are isolated, preventing them from experiencing a diversity of people, places, and activities, and dissociating them from much of mainstream society. The result for many living on the fringe is a decline in what we call "community," a sense of belonging to a place.

It is becoming increasingly clear that many Americans are clamoring for the kinds of changes in our development patterns that this chapter espouses for environmental, economic, and social sustainability. A 2004 nationwide public opinion poll conducted for the National Association of Realtors and Smart Growth America shows decisively that, while many of us continue to want single-family houses on green lots, we do not want them in a sprawling form. According to the opinion research firm Belden Russanello & Stewart, the 1,130 survey respondents voiced three main points:

• Americans favor smart growth communities with shorter commute times, sidewalks, and places to walk more than sprawling communities.

• The length of their commute to work holds a dominant place in Americans' decisions about where to live. Americans place a high value on limiting their commute times and they are more likely to see improved public transportation and changing patterns of housing development as the solutions to longer commutes than increasing road capacities.

• Americans want government and business to invest in existing communities before putting resources into newer communities farther out from cities and older suburbs. The public's priorities for development include more housing for people with moderate and low incomes and slowing the rate of development of open space. Many Americans also express the desire for more places to walk or bike in their communities.[44]

Fortunately for us, the American Dream need not become a runaway, and we need not flee our circumstances. We must, however, heed them. We could do a lot worse than to follow the eloquent admonition of Tony Hiss, in his wonderful book *The Experience of Place*:

> Make sure that when we change a place, the change agreed upon nurtures our growth as capable and responsible people while also protecting the natural environment and developing jobs and homes enough for all.[45]

We in the community of Americans can do that, and we can adopt a system of policies and practices to put it into effect. Indeed, we must.

NOTES

1. The author wishes to express his profuse gratitude to a number of colleagues and fellow travelers whose work has enriched this chapter: Laura Bruce, whose outstanding and thorough research has helped keep the facts and references up to date; Deron Lovaas, for the use of his own excellent writings on this subject, from which I have borrowed; and Michael Replogle, Matthew Raimi, Don Chen, Jutka Terris, and Nancy Vorsanger for their previous work with me on joint writings that have been adapted for parts of this chapter.

2. Population is projected to grow by 39.6 percent over 25 years, while converted land is projected to grow by 104 percent. Moreover, of the 1.2 million new residents of central Maryland in the mid-1990s, about a third (some 425,000 persons) represented out-migration from nearby cities. See Karl Blankenship, "Chewing Up the Landscape," *Bay Journal*, Baltimore: Chesapeake Bay Foundation, December 1995.

3. Henry L. Diamond and Patrick F. Noonan, *Land Use in America*, Washington, D.C.: Island Press, 1996. See also Rutherford H. Platt, *Land Use and Society*. Washington, D.C.: Island Press, 1996, pp. 138–39.

4. Anthony Downs, *Stuck In Traffic*, Washington, D.C.: The Brookings Institution; and Cambridge, Mass.: Lincoln Institute of Land Policy, 1992, pp. 18–19.

5. Mike Flagg and Neil Irwin, "Outer Suburbs' Job Boom," *The Washington Post*, October 27, 2004 (citing data from the federal Labor Department). The top 10 counties by job growth were overwhelmingly suburban and located either in the Southwest or Florida: In addition to those around Los Angeles, the list includes Clark in Nevada (Las Vegas), Maricopa in Arizona (outside Phoenix), Fairfax in Virginia (west of Washington), Hillsborough and Orange in Florida (outside Tampa and Orlando), and San Diego County in California.

6. Garreau, author of the classic 1991 book *Edge City: Life on the New Frontier*, is quoted in Rutherford H. Platt, *Land Use and Society*, Washington, D.C.: Island Press, 1996, pp. 138–39.

7. Reid Ewing, Rolf Pendall, and Don Chen,. *Measuring Sprawl and its Impacts*, Smart Growth America, 2002.

8. United Nations Centre for Human Settlements and the World Bank, Housing Indicators Program, Vol. III Preliminary Findings, New York: United Nations, 1993.

9. See College of Business Administration, University of Cincinnati, *Property Newsletter*, September 2000.

10. See Frank Jossi, "Rewrapping the Big Box," *Planning*, August 1998, p. 16.

11. Bureau of Transportation Statistics, U.S. Department of Transportation, *National Transportation Statistics 2003.*

12. See John Holtzclaw, et al, "Location Efficiency: Neighborhood and Socio-Economic Characteristics Determine Auto Ownership and Use: Studies in Chicago, Los Angeles, and San Francisco," *Transportation Planning and Technology*, Vol. 25, 2002; Michael Bernick and Robert Cervero, *Transit Villages In the 21st Century*, New York: McGraw-Hill, 1997. Susan Handy, *How Land Use Patterns Affect Travel Patterns: A Bibliography*, Council of Planning Librarians, 1992. In a more recent study, Handy suggests that it may not be density *per se* but its by-product accessibility (close access to frequent destinations) that leads to a reduction in driving and a corresponding increase in walking and bicycling. Susan Handy, *Critical Assessment of the Literature on the Relationships Among Transportation, Land Use, and Physical Activity*, Paper prepared for the Transportation Research Board and the Institute of Medicine Committee on Physical Activity, Health, Transportation, and Land Use (TRB Special Report 282), 2005.

13. Surface Transportation Policy Project, *High Mileage Moms* (1999).

14. Tom Lewis, *Divided Highways: Building the Interstate Highways, Transforming American Life*, New York: Viking, 1997.

15. Peter Newman and Jeffrey Kenworthy, *Cities and Sustainability*, Washington, D.C.: Island Press, 1999.

16. Remarks of Alan Greenspan to the Italian American Foundation, Washington, D.C., October 15, 2004, at www.federalreserve.com.

17. International Panel on Climate Change, *Summary for Policymakers of the Contribution of Working Group I to the IPCC Second Assessment Report*, 1995.

18. Office of Mobile Sources, U.S. Environmental Protection Agency, *Motor Vehicles and the 1990 Clean Air Act*, Fact Sheet OMS-11, August 1994.

19. U.S. Department of Transportation, Bureau of Transportation Statistics, *National Transportation Statistics 2003.*

20. Surface Transportation Policy Project, *Clearing the Air*, 2003.

21. U.S. Environmental Protection Agency, *Our Built and Natural Environments: A Technical Review of the Interactions Between Land Use, Transportation, and Environmental Quality*, EPA 231-R-01-002, January 2001, p. 26.

22. U.S. Department of Transportation, Federal Highway Administration, *Transportation Air Quality: Selected Facts and Figures*, FHWA-PD-96-006, 1996, p. 19.

23. Surface Transportation Policy Project, *Clearing the Air*, op. cit.

24. Ibid.

25. Reid Ewing and Barbara A. McCann, *Measuring the Health Effects of Sprawl*, Smart Growth America and Surface Transportation Policy Project, 2003. See also Sally Squires, "Chew Vaccine: The Anti-Flu Diet," *The Washington Post*, November 2, 2004, p. F1 (citing David Nieman, professor of health and exercise science at Appalachian State University). Susan Handy's work shows that physical activity increases in accessible, mixed use neighborhoods. Handy, Critical Assessment of the Literature on the Relationships Among Transportation, Land Use, and Physical Activity, op. cit.; Rajamani, Bhat, Handy, Knaap, and Song, *Assessing the Impact of Urban Form Measures in Nonwork Trip Mode Choice After Controlling for Demographic and Level-of-Service Effects*, TRB Paper 03-3392 (monograph), 2002.

26. See American Farmland Trust, *Farming On the Edge: Sprawling Development Threatens America's Best Farmland*, maintained at www.farmland.org/farmingontheedge/index.htm.

27. See U.S. Fish & Wildlife Service, *2000 Report Summary Findings, National Wetlands Inventory*, 2000, and *Report to Congress on the Status and Trends of Wetlands in the Conterminous United States 1986 to 1997*, available at http://wetlands.fws.gov/statusandtrends.htm.

28. State-by-state data are available in many sources, including the excellent summary: Reed F. Noss, and Robert L. Peters, *Endangered Ecosystems: A Status Report on America's Vanishing Habitat and Wildlife*, Defenders of Wildlife, 1995.

29. See National Wildlife Federation, *Rebuild It Right*, statement by NWF board chair Jerome Ringo, September 9, 2005, www.nwf.org/nwfwebadmin/binaryVault/09-09-05 _Katrina%20statement_Final.pdf.

30. Jonathan M. Harbor, "A Practical Method for Estimating the Impact of Land Use Change in Surface Runoff, Groundwater Recharge and Wetland Hydrology," *Journal of the American Planning Association*, Vol. 60, 1994, pp. 95–108.

31. Office of Policy, Planning and Evaluation, U.S. Environmental Protection Agency, *$mart Investments for City and County Managers: Energy, Environment, and Community Development*, Publication No. EPA-231-R-98-004, Washington, D.C.: U.S. Environmental Protection Agency, April 1998.

32. Southern California Association of Governments, *Preliminary Draft '97 Regional Transportation Plan*, Los Angeles: Southern California Association of Governments, 1997, p. 49.

33. Chris Lester and Jeffrey Spivak, "Road System Puts Suburbs on the Map," *The Kansas City Star*, December 19, 1995.

34. Tom Horton, "A Fumbling Approach to Growth," *The Baltimore Sun*, December 8, 1995, p. 2C.

35. See discussion and sources cited in F. Kaid Benfield et al., *Once There Were Greenfields*, New York: Natural Resources Defense Council, 1999, pp. 112–15.

36. Robert W. Burchell et al., *Costs of Sprawl-2000*, National Research Council, Transportation Research Board, Transit Cooperative Research Program, TCRP Report 74, 2002.

37. Surface Transportation Policy Project, *Driven to Spend: The Impact of Sprawl on Household Transportation Expenses*, 2000.

38. Mark Muro and Robert Puentes, *Investing in a Better Future: A Review of the Fiscal and Competitive Advantages of Smarter Growth Development Patterns*, Brookings Institution Center on Urban and Metropolitan Policy, 2004.

39. Jeremy Rifkin, "America, Wake Up to the European Dream," *The Washington Post*, October 31, 2004, p. B4.

40. See discussion and sources cited in Benfield et al., *Once There Were Greenfields*, op. cit., at pp. 121–22.

41. Brian Burnes, "The Interstate Changed Our Lives," *The Kansas City Star*, September 3, 1996.

42. Muro and Puentes, op. cit.

43. F. Kaid Benfield, Matthew D. Raimi, and Don Chen, *Once There Were Greenfields*, op. cit., p. 129 (citing James Howard Kunstler).

44. Belden Russanello & Stewart, 2004 American Community Survey/National Survey on Communities, Conducted for Smart Growth America and National Association of Realtors, 2004.

45. Tony Hiss, *The Experience of Place*, New York: Alfred A. Knopf, 1990, p. xii.

4

Transportation in the Multi-City Regions

Shelley Poticha[1]

Many of the major cities in Europe are connected by high-speed rail today, and all of them will be by 2020. Japan's major cities are connected by high-speed rail, and the Japanese continue to work to improve the speed and efficiency of rail travel. Taiwan is building a high-speed rail network to connect its major cities. In China work is underway to build high-speed railways linking Beijing to Shanghai, Nanjing, and other population centers. All of the cities that have high-speed rail also have airports; they all have a network of limited-access highways, and they all have local rail transit systems. Our global competitors have decided that high-speed rail is an essential element of a balanced transportation system.

A high-speed rail connection between Los Angeles and New York, or even Chicago and New York, will never be faster than flying. Distances between major cities in Japan, Taiwan, or Western Europe are much shorter. However, the multi-city regions are comparable in scale and density to Europe and Japan. While connections between these regions need to be made by air, many of the connections within these regions can be made by train.

CURRENT U.S. PLANS FOR HIGH-SPEED RAIL

The closest the U.S. comes to having high-speed rail at present is Amtrak's Acela service between Washington and Boston. The level of comfort and the appearance of the cars are somewhat similar to high-speed trains in

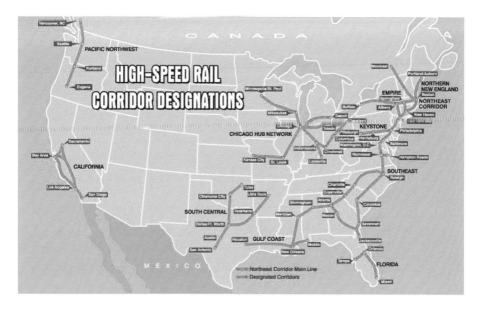

Fig. 4-1: The 11 High-Speed Rail Corridors designated by the Federal Railroad Administration.

Europe and Japan, but, because Acela operates on conventional tracks and shares the right-of-way with many other trains, the average speed along the entire route is only about 70 miles per hour. Even at these speeds, Acela, and the entire Amtrak system, are strong competitors not only with car travel but with airline travel from New York City to Washington or between intermediate stops along the route, if travel time is calculated from city center to city center. The total number of people currently riding trains between Washington and New York City is equivalent to all those flying the same route.

The Federal Railroad Administration has designated 11 high-speed rail corridors. They would serve all the multi-city regions discussed in Chapter 2 except the region we are calling the Inter-Mountain West. [Figure 4-1] High-speed rail is defined in the U.S. as rail that is time competitive with air or automobile travel at distances of 100 to 500 miles.[2] Sample trips of this distance include San Francisco to Los Angeles (380 miles), New York City to Washington, D.C. (232 miles), and Chicago to Minneapolis (409 miles).

California is pursuing plans to build a 700-mile high-speed rail system (the most ambitious in the U.S.). The idea would be to attain 220 miles per hour, which would produce average speeds comparable to high-speed rail lines in Europe. The California High-Speed Rail Authority, created in 1996, has been working to design and fund a system that will connect San Diego to Los Angeles, San Francisco, and Sacramento and that will be competitive in speed and service with airline travel and be faster and more convenient than travel by car. [Figure 4-2]

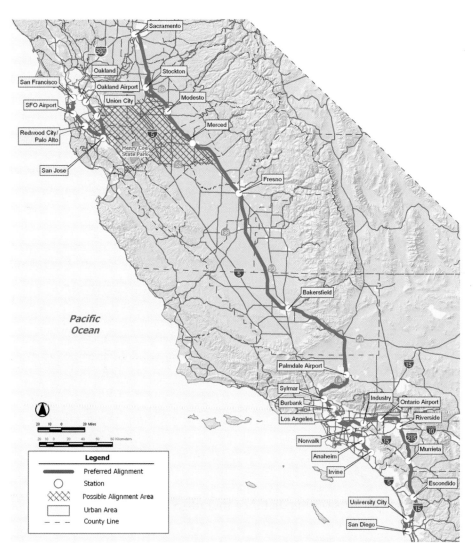

Fig. 4-2: Preferred High-Speed Rail Alignments and Stations Statewide as proposed by the California High-Speed Rail Authority.

In the fast-growing California region, high-speed rail would be cheaper than accommodating projected growth in travel demand with more highways and more air service. Californians currently make over 154 million annual trips between the state's major metropolitan regions. Over 42 million of these trips are for journeys at least 150 miles long. To accommodate the projected growth in demand, the state would need to build two new international airports and almost 3,000 additional lane-miles on intercity highways statewide.[3] While requiring a large investment in new rail infrastructure, the California high-speed rail project also has by far the largest market potential of all the U.S. corridors. The high-speed rail system is projected to carry 42 million passengers in 2020 and serve 45 percent of the current airline passengers.[4]

Two other states created ambitious plans comparable to California's but later gave them up. Texas in 1991 awarded a franchise to a private group to construct a high-speed rail to link Houston, Dallas-Fort Worth, and San Antonio. Political opposition from the airlines led the state to cancel the franchise three years later. The accompanying map is one version of what could have happened. [Figure 4-3]

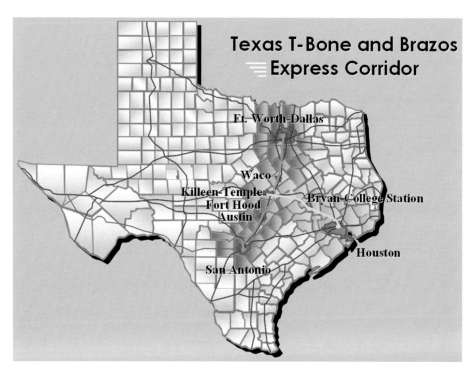

Fig. 4-3: One possible way to link major Texas cities by high-speed rail.

In Florida, voters approved a state constitutional amendment in 2000 that mandated a statewide high-speed rail system, and the Florida High-Speed Rail Authority was enacted by the legislature to plan and implement the system. In 2004 the voters repealed the constitutional amendment. The authority still exists, and has used federal grant money it had already obtained to complete a study of the first link, between Tampa and Orlando, and to study a link between Orlando and Miami. However, the authority is no longer receiving state funds and depends on federal grant money and potential interest by private investors.

Other states are focusing on upgrading existing railways for systems that would be competitive with automobile travel, rather than seeking to attain speeds such as those projected for California. However, given today's security requirements and endemic air traffic delays, a three- or four-hour train trip can be competitive with a one- or two-hour flight on a door-to-door basis.

Virginia, North Carolina, South Carolina, and Georgia have formed a four-state coalition to plan, develop, and implement high-speed rail in the Southeast. The system, running from Washington, D.C., to Atlanta, is being planned and developed incrementally using upgraded existing rail rights-of-way. Service might start in 2012 at the earliest. A trip from Charlotte to Washington, D.C., a straight line distance of 332 miles, is estimated to take between six and seven hours on the new service, which means an average speed of around 50 miles an hour, not as fast as Amtrak's Acela, and certainly not comparable to high-speed rail in Europe or Japan. Estimates for reconstructing, upgrading, and building the rail lines between Washington and Charlotte are $2.6 billion, about one-third less per mile than interstate highway improvements for a similar distance. The Charlotte-to-Raleigh segment (between two and three hours) and the Raleigh-to-Richmond and Richmond-to-Washington segments (both about two hours) are likely to attract more travelers than the complete trip because air travel would still have a big advantage over the longer haul. The segments from Atlanta to Charlotte are still in early planning stages, and comparable projections for these links are not yet available.

The Midwest Regional Rail Initiative is a cooperative effort among Amtrak, the Federal Railroad Administration, and nine states (Illinois, Indiana, Iowa, Michigan, Minnesota, Missouri, Nebraska, Ohio, and Wisconsin) to develop an improved and expanded passenger rail system

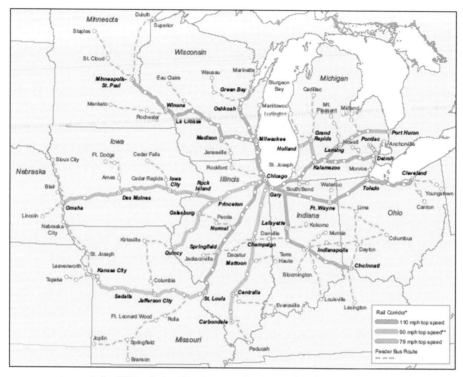

*Indiana DOT is evaluating additional passenger rail service to South Bend and to Louisville.
**In Missouri, current restrictions limit train speeds to 79 mph.

*Fig. 4-4: Route map of train improvements that comprise the Midwest
Regional Rail Initiative.*

in the Midwest. Trains operating at top speeds of 79, 90, and 110 miles
per hour—comparable to Amtrak's Acela—would link Chicago to many
Midwest locations through a hub-and-spoke system.[5] [Figure 4-4] The
Chicago-to-Detroit trip, now six hours, would take less than four. Chicago to the Twin Cities, now eight hours plus, would take less than six.
St. Louis to Kansas City would go from five and a half hours to less than
four hours. The nearly nine-hour Chicago-to-Cincinnati and Chicago-
to-Cleveland train trips would be cut in half.

These efficiencies would be achieved through improved train commu-
nication and control systems, enhancements to highway and railroad
grade crossing safety, rehabilitation of existing tracks, and construction of
new track and siding. In addition to travel time reductions, the system
would offer additional service—as many as 17 daily round trips between
Chicago and Milwaukee (including Amtrak's current long-distance

trains). Ridership on the entire system is projected to go up from the current 1.5 million passengers per year to 9.6 million per year.

The 2004 estimate for total capital investment, including infrastructure and rolling stock, was $7.7 billion, of which $1.1 billion would be for 63 new train sets that would provide Acela-style facilities. Infrastructure improvements are estimated to be about $2.2 million per mile. This compares favorably with typical highway costs of $10 million per mile.[6]

The funding plan consists of a mix of funding sources including federal loans and grants, state funding, and capital and revenue generated from system-related activities, such as joint development proceeds. Federal funding will be the primary source of capital funds. The system is projected to be self-supporting from fares.

The Amtrak Cascades train that links Eugene, Oregon, to Portland and Seattle, with connections through Everett and Bellingham to Vancouver, British Columbia, is a project of the states of Oregon and Washington in cooperation with Amtrak and the Federal Railroad Administration. The service uses five Spanish-built Talgo trains, somewhat similar to the Talgo trains used for high-speed rail service in Spain. The goal of the system is to be able to make the 310-mile trip from Eugene to Seattle in two and a half hours and to make the 156-mile trip from Seattle to Vancouver, where the terrain is more difficult, in just under three hours.

New York State has begun some preliminary work on developing higher speed and more frequent passenger rail service from New York City through Albany and Rensselaer to Buffalo.

Altogether, 34 states are participating in the development of some kind of rail corridor improvement. Except for California, and the ill-fated efforts in Texas and Florida, all these state investments, and the much larger federal investments, are aimed at getting people out of cars and onto trains. The argument in favor of funding is that these rail lines cost less on a per mile basis than interstate highways, and are much more energy efficient and cost efficient on a per passenger basis. The counter argument, made against all train and transit travel, is that you can never persuade highly individualistic Americans to give up their cars for long trips.

TRAINS AS AN ALTERNATIVE TO PLANES

What about giving Americans an alternative to air travel? U.S. airports are nearing saturation. More than half of all flights in and out of U.S. airports are less than 500 miles. [Figures 4-5, page 52]

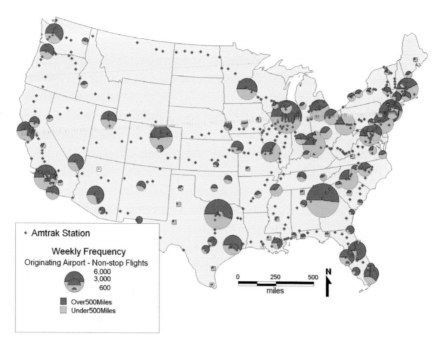

Fig. 4-5: The proportion of flights of less than 500 miles operating from major airports across the U.S.

When you take into account the time spent going to the airport, the time needed to go through security and board the plane, the flight itself, plus the trip to the actual destination from the airport, the door-to-door time for a short airplane trip today is often longer than it would be by conventional ground transportation: train, bus, or private car. And this calculation is made assuming no air-traffic delays. Anyone who travels frequently by air knows that a trip without delays is more and more unusual. If people making connections through the hub-and-spoke system of a major airport could connect through inter-city rail, part of the trip could be made by train. Getting these trips out of the demand for runways, gates, and air space could ease airport congestion. Airport operations appear to be subject to the tipping point theory. Above a certain number of planes per hour, the likelihood of congestion increases, and the problems caused by bad weather get progressively worse.

Despite proximity to nearby rail service, most U.S. airports do not have inter-city rail connections. Two exceptions are New Jersey's Newark International Liberty Airport and Baltimore Washington International Airport in Maryland. A travel port is an airport directly connected to inter-city rail and with a close connection to the national highway system, like Schiphol in the Netherlands. There is an inherent market for a national travel port system in the U.S. It is estimated that 99 percent of the U.S. population could be within 500 miles of an intermodal travel port and 84 percent could be within 200 miles.

A travel port system, by integrating rail service with airports, would allow some of the spokes of each airport's hub-and-spoke system to consist of trains instead of planes, a concept that could dramatically reduce air traffic congestion across the U.S.

There are other ways to reduce airport congestion: charging airlines a premium for gates at peak hours, routing planes to alternate airports such as Providence (instead of Boston) or Oakland (instead of San Francisco), or adding a runway. Another runway can improve airport capacity at the most congested central airports, but, in addition to the high cost of such improvements, there is often formidable political opposition from people who fear the effects of a new flight path.

If a rail option can reduce airport congestion at a cost equal to, or less than, the cost of adding runways or building additional terminals or airports, high-speed rail could be an effective substitute for some of the new airports or new runways that will be needed to reduce airport congestion—thereby justifying the cost of rail construction even before one considers other beneficial effects.

Consider a hypothetical travel port system. Suppose Chicago's O'Hare International Airport were linked to the proposed Midwest Regional Rail Initiative. O'Hare is one of the world's busiest international airports. It is often congested and has little room for expansion. However, the Chicago area could generate a significant number of rail and bus travelers; there are several medium-sized cities within a radius of 200 to 400 miles, and there is considerable intercity travel within this travel shed by both auto and air. The map [Figure 4-6, page 54] shows these markets, home to over 5.3 million people, and the number of annual flights that serve them directly from O'Hare.

While more than half of O'Hare's one million annual landings and take-offs[7] are for trips longer than 400 miles, some 28,000 airline trips in the region could be displaced by the high-speed rail system.[8] With less susceptibility to weather and other kinds of delays facing airlines, high-speed regional rail would be an important travel option.

Regional rail would serve three types of customers currently traveling by air. Rail would replace certain city-to-city trips within the Midwest; it

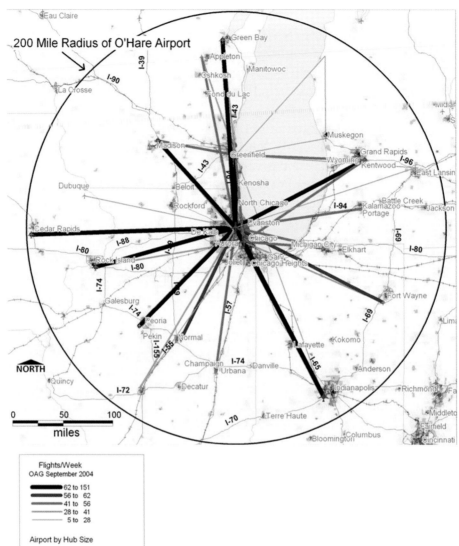

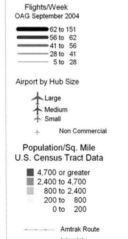

Fig. 4-6: Weekly flights within a 200-mile radius of O'Hare International Airport, all of which could be accomplished more efficiently by high-speed rail if there were direct connections.

would replace some "spoke" trips for passengers flying through Chicago; and it would serve passengers arriving or departing at O'Hare who could ride the train instead of driving to the airport. This range of travel services would contribute to the 13.6 million projected rail passengers per year by 2025.[9]

Europe's high-speed trains are beginning to be integrated with airports. The Thalys system of high-speed rail lines connects Paris to Belgium and the Netherlands, and it connects to Charles de Gaulle International Airport near Paris. Air France no longer flies between De Gaulle and Brussels; it books its connecting passengers on Thalys. Other airlines also have code-sharing arrangements that permit flights and Thalys train trips to be booked as one ticket to or from Charles de Gaulle Airport, Schiphol Airport in the Netherlands, and other destinations between Paris and Amsterdam. In the U.S., Continental Airlines will ticket flights to and from Newark airport to Northeast corridor destinations via Amtrak.

TRANSIT CAN GIVE STRUCTURE TO REGIONAL DEVELOPMENT

Automobiles promote dispersed development, but trains promote compact, concentrated development around stops along the system. Airports also promote concentrated development. Together the two are a potent combination. Integrating airports and rail systems does more than reduce congestion; its build up the airport as a regional urban location. Schiphol Airport is a good example. There is frequent passenger service to Schiphol from all the principal cities in the Netherlands, in addition to the connection to the Thalys high-speed rail system between Amsterdam, Brussels, and Paris. These rail connections, combined with good highway access, are helping to make Schiphol into an economic center, comparable to the traditional downtown of a major city. In addition to the passenger and cargo facilities found at all big airports, and the hotels and retail now being added to airports almost everywhere, Schiphol is also an office center where one can walk from the arrival and departures hall, or the adjacent train station, to space in major office buildings within 10 minutes. There are business parks with office space close to Schiphol, as there are at other major airports; it is the direct walkable connection between office space and the airport that is similar to a traditional downtown. That link is a direct result of the rail connections.

High-speed rail linked to airports will be even more effective as a transportation system if there are good connections between high-speed rail stations and local rail-transit systems at each stop. This capability already exists with the Washington Metro and with older rapid transit systems at many of the stops on Amtrak's Northeast corridor. New rail transit systems in other parts of the country have been much more successful than expected at attracting ridership, but only now are experts realizing how important these systems are as a way to link local areas with national and international air travel.

A location on a rapid-transit stop also creates opportunities for compact, mixed use, walkable communities, and it turns out that there is a market for living in such places. A recent study by the Center for Transit Oriented Development found that more than 16 million households will want to live near transit by 2030. Some of these communities have been designed as traditional towns within auto-oriented suburbs, but there are now many examples of successful compact, mixed use developments in suburban downtowns located on commuter lines, and comparable development around stops on some of the new transit lines being developed in places like Dallas that did not have a strong commuter rail system in the past. As of 2006, Minneapolis had seen more than 7,000 housing units spring up around the Hiawatha light rail line, which opened in 2004. In the Denver region, more than 13,000 units are planned for the T-REX light rail line expansion scheduled to open in late 2006. Some of these station areas have become brand names in themselves. Mockingbird station in Dallas is a prime example of how transit can encourage a sense of place.

The poster city for transit-oriented development continues to be metropolitan Portland, Oregon, where rapid transit was selected in preference to building new highway corridors. With the help of multi-modal transit planning and development agreements, downtown Portland has been transformed into a walkable mix of residences, offices, shops, and entertainment. The seamless integration of Portland State University, downtown Portland, and the Pearl District by streetcar has begun to redefine how we think about the purpose of specific transit modes. Compact development has grown up around some of Portland's suburban transit stops, and the long-range Portland regional plan calls for more intense, transit-oriented development at transit stations instead of the spread of urban areas outward into prime agricultural land. Metropolitan Portland's planning policy has been underpinned by urban growth boundary legislation, which is now in question because of the success of a recent property rights referendum. It may be that the location incentives created by transit can continue to promote these policies with less reliance on land-use controls.

Transit systems also can link the multiple urban centers that grow up in today's dispersed urban regions. Minneapolis's Hiawatha line connects the Mall of America, the airport, the veterans' hospital, and downtown Minneapolis—together producing ridership that has already exceeded 2020 goals. Houston's Metrorail has also exceeded its ridership predictions; that system connects downtown and three major sports stadiums with Rice University and the world's largest medical district.

It is possible to look at stations and their location efficiencies. Reconnecting America, in a study completed in 2004, looked at demographic and transport patterns in "transit zones," defined as areas within a half-mile of existing transit stations in U.S. cities. The study found that households in transit zones own an average of 0.9 cars, compared to an average of 1.6 cars in the metro regions as a whole, most likely a lifestyle rather than a financial decision. Car ownership rates near Metro stations in Arlington County, Virginia, were found to be much lower than in the region as a whole, while average household income is higher than the regional average.

This study also found that automobile travel is much lower in transit zones. Some 54 percent of residents living in transit zones commute by car, compared to 83 percent in a region as a whole. More residents commute by car in the regions with small and medium-sized systems (72 percent and 77 percent, respectively) than in the large and extensive systems (65 percent and 49 percent, respectively). The regions with the lowest percentage of residents commuting by car are New York (36 percent), Washington D.C. (54 percent), and Seattle (54 percent), all of which have relatively extensive transit networks. The regions with transit systems where the highest percentage of residents commute by car are Memphis and Dallas (both 86 percent), Tampa (79 percent) and Sacramento (89 percent)—all cities with newer, smaller, transit networks.

Recognizing the effect of transit on travel behavior and car ownership leads to the concept of the housing and transportation affordability index. Housing affordability is often measured as a percentage of household income. The number accepted by home mortgage lenders is 30 percent. But the location of housing can have large indirect effects on transportation costs—in the ownership and maintenance of private automobiles and in time and money spent to access jobs and services. While housing prices in urban, mixed use communities are often higher than in outlying regions, transportation costs can be below 10 percent of household income, while in suburban areas that number is often 25 percent.

Average Americans spend 19 percent of their budget on transportation. Combining housing and transportation into an affordability index provides households and policy makers a better idea of the costs associated with various housing options and how they affect family budget decisions.[10]

Because there is a strong market for living space in compact, urban environments with good access to transit, it is reasonable to expect that some proportion of a regional population will choose to live in such areas in the future, without expecting people to give up their cars and their suburban houses if they don't want to.

Residential densities of seven to nine units per net acre can support bus rapid transit. That translates to an average lot size of 5,000 to 6,000 square feet—a suburban single-family lot 50 feet by 100 feet fits this specification. Twenty-five employees per net acre would be a comparable minimum for a commercial district. Twelve units per acre, implying attached town houses or zero lot line patio houses, will support a full-scale rail rapid transit system. A four-story office building with a standard floor plan generally has at least 100 employees per floor. Such a building covers a little more than half an acre. One every eight acres would support rail rapid transit.

These are not urban densities. And these are just averages: Individual locations could have lower densities as long as the necessary average is achieved with a few bigger buildings. We are not talking about most people living in small urban flats, and working on canyon-like streets, in order to have transit.

The density of most new development today does not support any kind of rapid transit. A net residential density of four units to the acre is unusual, and gross densities of less than two families per acre are the norm in new development, as shown in Chapter 2. Employment is also becoming more and more dispersed. As Robert Lang (of the Metropolitan Institute of Virginia Tech) has observed, the relatively compact edge cities of 15 or 20 years ago, located at highway interchanges near major airports and perceived at the time as a radical form of decentralization, have given way to what he calls edgeless cities, a far more diffuse development pattern for some 37 percent of new office development that is spread out over tens or even hundreds of square miles.

High-speed rail that links the urban centers and airports of each multi-city region would be an antidote to the formless spread of urbanization, because the station stops along the high-speed rail lines would be the gateways to the global economy. Each stop would be a preferred location for any business that needs access to long-distance transportation. There would be stops at the airports, supporting the development of new airport cities, and in the biggest existing development concentrations, whether they are traditional downtowns or newer edge cities. There is obviously a trade-off between speed and the number of stops, so these new central locations would always have to be limited in number. They would each be supported by a network of local transit systems.

The rationale for investing in rapid transit to support central development locations is not to compete with highways, but to create a more affordable pattern of development. Urbanizing greenfield land at the edge of a metropolitan area costs from $60,000 to $100,000 an acre in new infrastructure costs, taking into account only the necessary regrading of the landscape, the building of access roads, and the provision of utilities. Building at higher densities in already developed areas by providing rapid transit can mean no additional infrastructure costs, or costs per acre of $10,000 to $20,000. The money saved by not investing in infrastructure at the metropolitan fringe can more than offset the investment in rapid transit.

This comparison assumes that the area population is increasing, and that the cost of providing schools and other services for an increased number of people would be the same in either location. In metropolitan areas like Cleveland or St. Louis, which are seeing rapid growth with little or no increase in metropolitan population, the savings from building transit would be greater, because existing services would be used more efficiently.

In summary, it makes sense to pay for high-speed rail to link urban centers and airports within each multi-city region, in order to make better use of some of the money that will otherwise be spent on new airports, terminals, and runways. It makes sense to pay for rapid transit networks to bring people to urban centers, because the increased densities that can be supported along the transit corridors will draw some people away from developments on the urban fringe. Investing in this transit is more cost effective than continuing to build the inefficient road and utilities networks needed to support dispersed, low-density development. It is also more environmentally friendly, as airports produce some of the highest pollution levels in the U.S.

High-speed rail is needed to reinforce the downtowns and edge cities in the multi-city regions and make them major business destinations. Transit will be needed to bring people into these centers and to support compact, mixed use communities for which there is a strong, unmet market demand. This is the balanced transportation system that is being built in China and Taiwan, and that other global competitors in Europe and Japan already have.

Chapter 5 describes a case-study of how such a globally competitive transportation system could transform the seven-county Orlando region in Central Florida.

NOTES

1. Mariia Zimmerman, Scott Bernstein, Justin Fried, and Jeff Wood contributed to the content of this chapter.
2. U.S. Department of Transportation, Federal Railroad Administration. "High Speed Ground Transportation"; at www.fra.dot.gov/us/content/31.
3. California High-Speed Rail Authority and the Federal Railroad Administration, "A Plan to Fly California . . . without ever leaving the ground," Highlights from the Final Program Environmental Impact Report/Environmental Impact Statement for the Proposed California High-Speed Train System, 2005.
4. Center for Clean Air Policy and Center for Neighborhood Technology. "High Speed Rail and Greenhouse Gas Emissions in the U.S." January 2006; available at www.cnt.org/repository/HighSpeedRailEmissions.pdf.
5. Transportation Economics & Management Systems, Inc. "Midwest Regional Rail System: Executive Report." September 2004; at www.dot.state.wi.us/projects/state/docs/railmidwest.pdf.
6. Ibid. p. 14.
7. Based on Airports Council International survey. Total passengers enplaned and deplaned; passengers in transit counted once. Total movements based on total aircraft landing and take off.
8. Center for Clean Air Policy and Center for Neighborhood Technology. "High Speed Rail and Greenhouse Gas Emissions in the U.S." January 2006; at www.cnt.org/repository/HighSpeedRailEmissions.pdf.
9. Transportation Economics & Management Systems, Inc. "Midwest Regional Rail System: Executive Report." September 2004; at www.dot.state.wi.us/projects/state/docs/railmidwest.pdf.
10. The Affordability Index. Brookings Metropolitan Policy Program, 2006.

5

Alternate Futures for the Seven-County Orlando Region

Jonathan Barnett[1]

What should be the future of the rapidly growing seven-county Orlando region in central Florida? In 2000, myregion.org, an organization with the same name as its website, was formed to involve the largest possible constituency group in planning the region centered around Orlando. Eighteen public and private organizations were the original founders, with a convening role played by the Orlando Regional Chamber of Commerce.

An early step was to compile a source book of information about the region, as planning information in Florida is usually organized by county. The focus of the sourcebook, completed in 2003 by consultants Michael Gallis & Associates, was economic development in a global context. The sourcebook summarizes the findings and recommendations of more than 2,000 business, government, and civic leaders.

The next step was to look at the population projections for the future of the region, see where current growth trends were going, and consider whether there were better alternatives. The coordinator for this step was the Center for Metropolitan Studies at the University of Central Florida in Orlando, which turned to a research group from the Department of City and Regional Planning at the University of Pennsylvania to make a study of alternate futures for the region.

The Penn researchers were asked to provide two illustrations of what the seven-county region might look like in 2050. One was the trend model, a good-faith effort to show what would happen to the area if trends in population growth, transportation investments, employment, and development continued without major planning and policy changes. The alternative scenario would examine what the region might look like if there were concerted efforts to preserve the natural landscape, if there were a regional transit system tied to statewide high-speed rail, and if public policies encouraged higher development densities in places with good transit access and relatively favorable environmental impacts.

TREND SCENARIO:
POPULATION MORE THAN DOUBLES BY 2050

The University of Florida's Bureau of Economic and Business Research, BEBR, supplies population projections to Florida's government agencies, and it had made population projections for each of the seven counties to 2030. In order to prepare the trend and alternative models, the Penn study had to extend these projections to 2050. Of course, there is a large element of uncertainty looking so far into the future. There is uncertainty in such projections in the much nearer term as well: Osceola County has been growing faster than the BEBR mid-level estimates. Seminole County might run out of available land to accommodate the projected population at the assumed population densities by 2030. Would that "excess" growth go to other counties? Would it not take place at all? Would densities increase?

The study assumed that BEBR had a good grasp of the general trend, and that the region was a discrete unit where projected growth could be expected to stay within the seven-county area. The study therefore put the mid-range population growth projections for all seven counties together, used two methods of population projection to 2050, straight line and exponential, and averaged them.

The population of the region was 1.66 million in 1980, 2.4 million in 1990, and just over three million in 2000. In 2030 BEBR statistics project a regional population of 5.3 million, and the Penn Study projections to 2050 show a regional population of just over 7.2 million. Between the three million people living in the region in 2000 and the 7.2 million projected to live there in 2050 is an increase of 136 percent. These figures do not count the millions of visitors to the area's many tourist attractions. For people who feel that the Orlando region is already over-crowded, these numbers are eye-opening. Even if they are not totally accurate, they still give a good picture of the problems future growth will create for the Orlando region.

THE TREND MODEL:
RELATING POPULATION GROWTH TO LAND DEVELOPMENT

Where are the 4.2 million additional people going to live? In Florida, particularly because the state requires that development have supporting infrastructure in place when construction begins, new development is more likely to be close to existing urbanized areas. To some extent

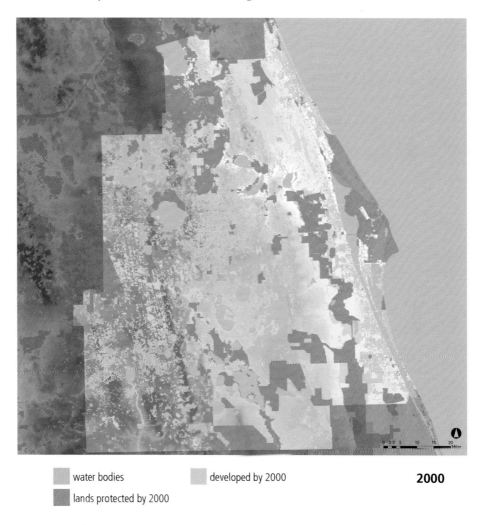

water bodies   developed by 2000   **2000**

lands protected by 2000

Fig. 5-1: The Seven County Orlando Region in 2000.

public policy will also direct growth away from wetlands and other environmentally sensitive areas. People prefer to live relatively close to work, so the major employment centers in the region, such as the airport, the theme parks, downtown Orlando, and the Kennedy Space Center at Cape Canaveral, can be expected to attract future development.

The study used ArcGIS 9.0 with the Spatial Analyst extension to create the trend model. This program allowed the land in the seven-county region to be ranked by its attractiveness for new development, based on such factors as proximity to existing development, attractive power of employment centers, and avoidance of wetlands. It was then

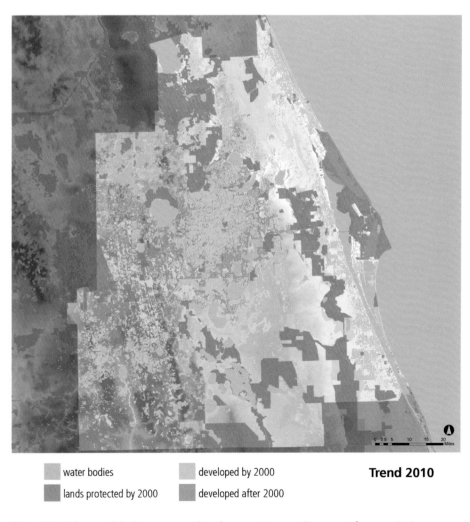

| water bodies | developed by 2000 | **Trend 2010** |
| lands protected by 2000 | developed after 2000 | |

Fig. 5-2: The model shows new development spreading out from existing built areas.

assumed that the projected new population would occupy the most attractive land.

The U.S. Geological Study Land Cover Analysis for 2000, based on satellite imagery, gives an accurate picture of existing development at the time of the census. [Figure 5-1] Data on the location of currently preserved open space in the region was obtained from the Nature Conservancy and the Florida Natural Lands Inventory.

The average household size across the seven counties in 2000 was 2.49 people. The study assumes that this number would hold constant to 2050, although household size in the region probably will decline, in

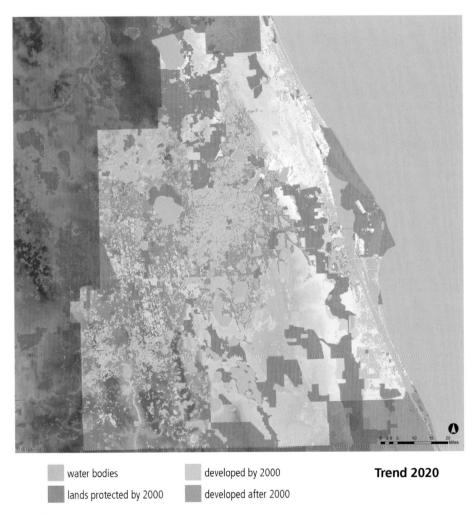

water bodies	developed by 2000	**Trend 2020**
lands protected by 2000	developed after 2000	

Fig. 5-3: The model shows low-density growth corridors forming to the northwest and southwest.

keeping with national trends. The study preferred to use conservative assumptions to avoid overstating anticipated problems.

In 2000 the average gross density in the region was 1.44 dwelling units per acre. Gross density is calculated by dividing all developed acres by the number of housing units, as recorded in the census. The category of developed acres includes all uses, not just residences. Another conservative assumption: The number of dwelling units per developed acre would also hold constant to 2050. Between 1993 and 2000, the average gross density of new development in the region was only 0.99, so the study could have postulated that gross densities would

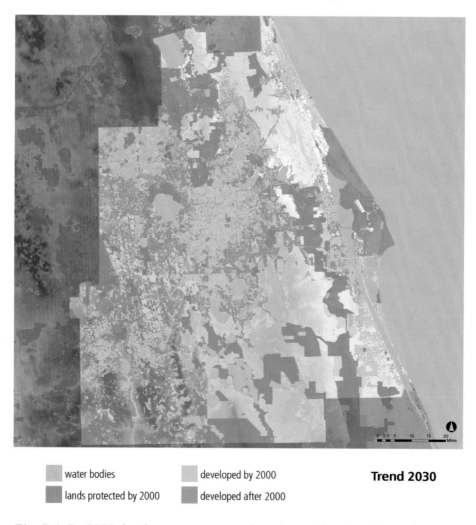

water bodies	developed by 2000
lands protected by 2000	developed after 2000

Trend 2030

Fig. 5-4: By 2030 development patterns show intensification of growth corridors and continuing loss of environmentally sensitive land.

decline from the 1.44 average in 2000. However, there will be compensating factors in the future, such as increasing difficulty in locating development parcels.

The study assumed there would be one household per dwelling unit, so that there would be a gross population density of new development of 1.44 times 2.49. That is approximately 3.6 persons per developed acre. This is the projected average gross population density of new development.

The purpose of the trend model was to map the extent of future growth. Using gross residential development density as a stand-in for all urbanization does not include predicting which parcels of land will

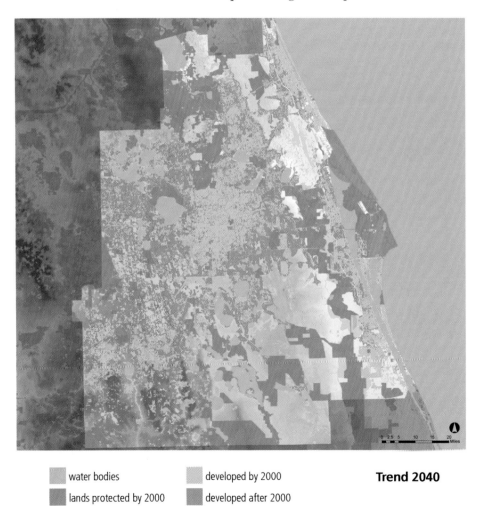

▨ water bodies	▨ developed by 2000
▨ lands protected by 2000	▨ developed after 2000

Trend 2040

Fig. 5-5: The trend continues: almost all the environmentally sensitive ridge land is built over; roads and highways are stressed beyond capacity.

be developed to what purpose. Office parks, shopping centers, and other activities are all part of the land developed at the gross residential density. The model therefore doesn't consider existing zoning mapped in undeveloped areas. Also the model extrapolates current trends. For example, it does not predict what would happen if parts of the region could not sustain the projected growth because water resources were depleted. The model assumed that automobiles will continue to be the dominant form of transportation and the existing freight distribution system will remain essentially the same. The model did not include future highway construction as an influence on location.

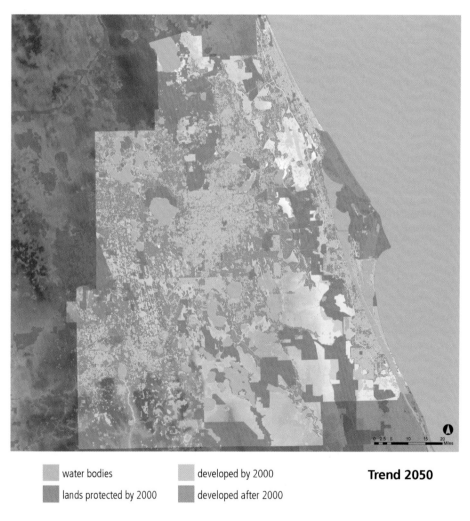

water bodies	developed by 2000	**Trend 2050**
lands protected by 2000	developed after 2000	

Fig. 5-6: By 2050 the trend is clearly unsustainable.

In summary the model is a projection, it is not a prediction.

The preceding five illustrations show the trend maps from 2000 to 2050 at 10-year intervals showing developed, developable, and remaining available land for each period. [Figures 5-2 to 5-6]

COSTS OF THE TREND MODEL

According to the trend model, 1.16 million acres of currently undeveloped land will need to be urbanized by 2050 to accommodate future population growth in the Orlando region, its associated economic activity, and local government facilities and infrastructure. The study estimated the cost of providing local roads, utilities, and other services to newly developed land in the seven-county region at $90,000 an acre, a cumulative cost of $104.7 billion.

Comparing the land marked as developed by 2050 in the trend model with maps of environmentally sensitive land shows that 610,971 acres, more than half the new urbanization, will over-run land that probably should not be developed at all. While it is impossible to put a dollar figure on this environmental cost, it is clearly a serious problem.

Some $8.3 billion dollars in highway improvements are currently programmed for the region up to 2025. Projecting the same per capita highway costs into the future, it is estimated that highway construction would cost a total of $12 billion up to 2050. The school costs associated with the population increase were estimated by the study as over $14 billion. Schools and highways were not included in the estimated costs of urbanization per acre. A rough estimate of development costs attributable to the trend model is $130.7 billion, an amount that excludes the costs of any actual buildings. This is a figure to keep in mind in looking at alternatives.

AN ALTERNATIVE TO THE TREND

The study then demonstrated one of the many potential alternatives to the trend. Just as the trend model is a projection, but not a prediction, the alternative model is an illustration of the ways in which the trend could be modified; it is not a plan for what should happen.

The study postulated three initiatives that together could transform the trend:

• Safeguarding significant natural resource areas from urbanization.

• Creating a rail transportation and transit system to supplement autos, buses, and trucks.

• Encouraging higher development densities in locations well served by transit.

The study identified four natural systems critical to the ecological balance of the region: the Ocala Forest; a zone of natural springs north of Orlando with a close connection to the aquifer, dunes, and coastal areas; and the crest line of the natural ridge land. In addition, the study postulated that there would be preemptive actions to acquire large contiguous tracts of property in the environmentally sensitive areas that

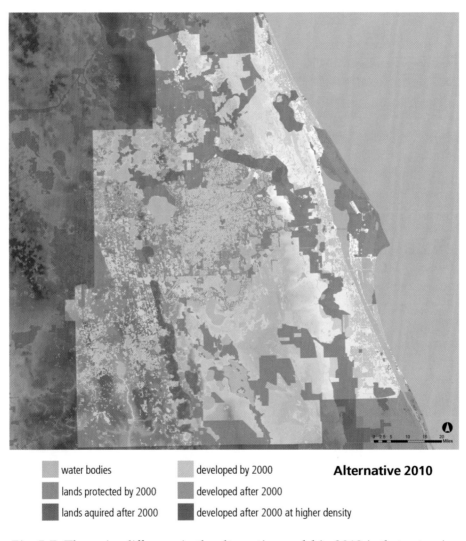

water bodies	developed by 2000	**Alternative 2010**
lands protected by 2000	developed after 2000	
lands aquired after 2000	developed after 2000 at higher density	

Fig. 5-7: The major difference in the alternative model in 2010 is that extensive areas of environmentally sensitive land have been preserved from development.

were clearly in the path of development—rather than relying on scattered proffers from property owners. The study assumed that average acquisition costs per acre would be $25,000, some 10 times more than usual payment for conservation land. An acquisition program was then devised in 10-year increments to 2050.

In 2000, Florida voters amended their constitution to require the creation of a statewide high-speed rail system. The amendment was repealed four years later, although the authority created to implement

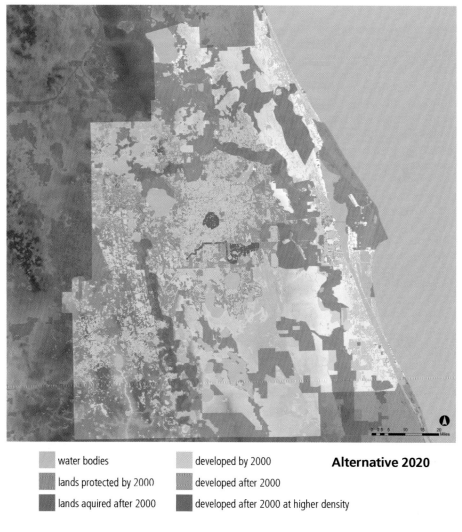

water bodies	developed by 2000	**Alternative 2020**
lands protected by 2000	developed after 2000	
lands aquired after 2000	developed after 2000 at higher density	

Fig. 5-8: By 2020 the alternative model shows more land preserved and the first transit oriented development beginning.

high-speed rail still exists. The study assumes that the high-speed rail system would ultimately be built, providing for connections between Orlando, other major centers in the region, and then Miami, Tampa, and Jacksonville. The study also took several plans for rapid transit that already existed and augmented them to create a regional transit system centered on Orlando. Because some of the transit would use a railway right-of-way currently used for freight, the study also postulated an alternative freight rail distribution system that had already been proposed by the area's Metropolitan Planning Organization.

water bodies	developed by 2000	**Alternative 2030**
lands protected by 2000	developed after 2000	
lands aquired after 2000	developed after 2000 at higher density	

Fig. 5-9: High-speed rail helps create denser development in downtown Orlando and at the airport; there is also denser development along transit corridors.

Finally, the international airport, downtown Orlando, Lakeland, San
ford, and Daytona Beach were assumed to be locations for major regional
centers by 2050 because they would be stops on the high-speed rail system, and there would be denser development around stops along the
transit corridors as well.

The computer model for the alternative began with land developed
in 2000 or already preserved from development, the same beginning
point as the trend model. However, for the alternative, it was postulated
that substantial areas of environmentally sensitive land would be pur-

water bodies	developed by 2000	**Alternative 2040**
lands protected by 2000	developed after 2000	
lands aquired after 2000	developed after 2000 at higher density	

*Fig. 5-10: By 2040 the full transit system is in place, and the last purchases
of preservation land are complete.*

chased during each 10-year period and thus would be unavailable for development and excluded from consideration in the model.

The areas around the high-speed rail stations were in effect zoned for higher density development, as were the stops along the transit corridors, although not as high a density as at the high-speed rail stations. This did not mean that all the land zoned for higher density was assumed to be developed. The higher density areas were only marked as developed if they were attractive enough within the parameters of the model to be developed.

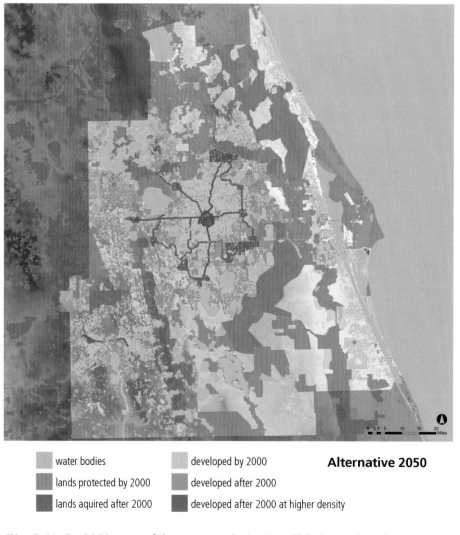

water bodies	developed by 2000	**Alternative 2050**
lands protected by 2000	developed after 2000	
lands aquired after 2000	developed after 2000 at higher density	

Fig. 5-11: By 2050 most of the area population is still living in low density areas but there are now higher density alternatives and much more efficient land use.

The preceding five illustrations show the alternative maps from 2000 to 2050 at 10-year intervals showing developed, developable, and remaining available land for each period. [Figures 5-7 to 5-11]

COSTS OF THE ALTERNATIVE MODEL

The computer model shows 420,410 newly developed acres, a 64 percent reduction over the trend model. Almost all the new urbanization, 408,555 acres, was on land categorized as environmentally sensitive in some way. However, there was a 53.8 percent reduction in urbanization of the land considered most sensitive, and a 67.7 percent reduction in the urbanization of the second most sensitive lands, with the urbanization of the next three categories reduced by more than half as well. Altogether, a third less environmentally sensitive land is shown as urbanized in the alternative model. Making all this possible is that 328,904 acres are shown as receiving some degree of more intense development.

The cost of urbanizing the 420,410 acres at $90,000 an acre would be $37.8 billion. The study estimated a cost of $20,000 an acre for new infrastructure associated with intensification of existing development, another $6.6 billion. The acquisition costs for 724,429 acres of environmentally sensitive land at an average cost of $25,000 an acre came to $18.1 billion. The regional share of high-speed rail, the new freight system, plus rapid transit and a proposed ferry system, came to $27.9 billion. The school costs remained the same at $14 billion.

The bottom line: The alternative model is projected to cost $26.3 billion less than the trend model, assuming that the costs of the actual buildings and landscaping would be similar under both scenarios. Perhaps more important, the maps make it clear that the region could go 20 years into the future along the conventional development path and find that it had invested in an unworkable and undesirable form of development, all the while destroying the environment that is a major reason why people are attracted to the Orlando region. Under the alternative, much of the existing development remains as it is, and conventional development continues as well. The highest residential densities shown are equivalent to what takes place in some sections of downtown Orlando today, about 50 dwelling units to the acre. The transit corridor densities are on the order of 12 units to the acre, so that the study is proposing more choices for people, but not a change in lifestyle for people who don't want to change.

Although everyone understands that the two models are full of assumptions, and that the specific acres and dollars are only illustrative, the basic message is clear. Big public policy decisions need to be made, and they need to be made soon. The organization called myregion.org is now engaged in a major community visioning process to build understanding and support for the hard choices ahead.

NOTES

1. The projections and maps in this chapter are based on a research studio at the University of Pennsylvania directed by Jonathan Barnett in the spring of 2005. The participants, now graduates, were Cate Brandt, Andrew Dobshinsky, Ilse Frank, Brad Goetz, Kathleen Grady, Thalia Husain, Kunbok Lee, Sarah Lovell, Herman Mao, Lauren Mosler, Andrew Nothstine, Abhay Pawar, Tyler Pollesch, Doug Robbins, and Jade Shipman. The sponsor for this studio was the Center for Metropolitan Studies at the University of Central Florida.

CHAPTER

6

Reinventing Megalopolis: The Northeast Megaregion

Robert D. Yaro and Armando Carbonell[1]

The Northeast megaregion was first identified by Jean Gottmann in his 1961 study, *Megalopolis*, as an "intense cluster of metropolitan areas" stretching from Virginia to Maine, that was "characterized by density of activities and movement," a description that holds true today.[2] In 1967 the transportation, economic, and environmental links of this region were further analyzed and mapped by the Regional Plan Association in *The Region's Growth*, prepared by RPA as part of its Second Regional Plan. RPA redefined the Northeast as "The Atlantic Urban Region," with an urban core largely as described by Gottmann, but added to this core the surrounding natural, agricultural, and scenic areas that provided the region's water supplies, food, and recreational opportunities.[3]

The activities and movements identified by Gottmann create overlapping functional regions, such as those shaped by commuting patterns, the movement of goods, the relationships between business headquarters and their branches, and the travel of residents between their homes and the places they vacation. Together, they help to define and redefine the megaregion as the flows of people, goods, and capital shift because of the global market and an increasingly technological society.

Despite decades of growth and development, the multi-city urban core of the Northeast is still largely the same as it was when defined by Gottmann and RPA four decades ago. [Figure 6-1, page 78] Comprised of the contiguous metropolitan areas of the five major cities—Boston,

77

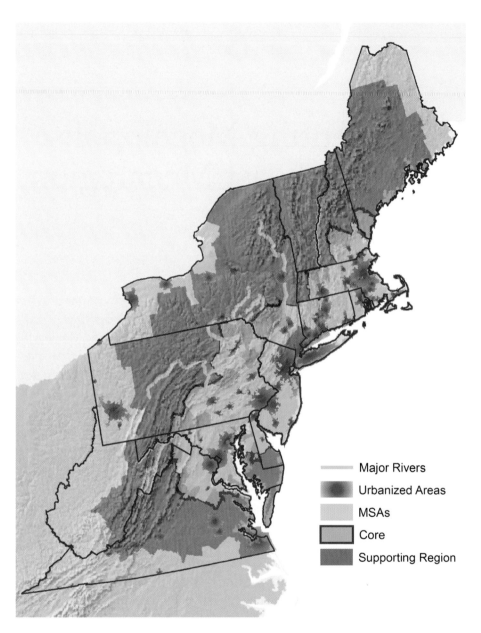

Fig. 6-1: The Northeast Megalopolis and its surrounding region.

New York City, Philadelphia, Baltimore, and Washington, D.C.—the urban core covers 61,634 square miles and represents only two percent of America's land area, yet is home to 49.5 million people, or almost 18 percent of the U.S. population in 2000. The urban core of the Northeast also produces 20 percent of the country's Gross Domestic Product (GDP). Taking land area into consideration, the Northeast urban core produces 10 times more GDP per square mile than the U.S. national average. The Northeast's economic output represents six percent of the world GDP. If the Northeast were an independent country, its economy would be larger than that of Germany or the United Kingdom.

The Northeast region's sense of place, its environmental quality, and its urban form have been shaped by its land forms and natural resource systems, principally the Appalachian Mountains, which form its western border, and the Atlantic Ocean to the east. Five major rivers—the Connecticut, Hudson, Delaware, Susquehanna, and Potomac—provided a setting for the region's early settlement, and continue to shape the development of the region's population centers.

With over 500 miles of Atlantic coastline, the Northeast's seacoast contains some of the nation's most popular and exclusive resorts, from the Maine coast to Cape Cod, from the Hamptons on Long Island to the Jersey and Maryland shores. Eleven estuaries, including Narragansett Bay, Long Island Sound, and the Chesapeake Bay, provide the region with unique ecological habitats, commercial and sport fisheries, and additional recreational and scenic resources. The five major rivers connect the mountains to the ocean and provide drinking water for more than 55 million people. Some of the country's most fertile farmland is situated in the Northeast, as well as 12 million acres of protected open space and parkland. These environmental assets help make the Northeast a desirable place to live and do business, and provide a pressure valve for the dense urbanization of the megaregion's urban core.

PRESERVING THE REGION'S COMPETITIVENESS

Despite the natural assets of the Northeast region, the strength of its transportation network, and the prominence and vibrancy of its leading cities, it is losing its competitive edge vis-à-vis the rest of the nation and the world. This loss of competitiveness is born out by the Northeast's declining share of GDP, its loss of top Fortune 500 companies, and growing economic and social disparities between successful cities or wealthy suburbs and bypassed urban centers, declining first-tier suburbs, and bypassed rural areas, particularly in the parts of Appalachia included in the region. These challenges are compounded by the higher tax burdens endured in the Northeast, as compared to the rest of the country. The whole region also has aging infrastructure systems that require increasing funding just for maintenance, not to mention expansion. Moreover, the region's economic potential and quality of life are threatened by growing congestion and escalating housing costs. Strategies aimed at growing the economy, accommodating new residents, and maintaining the Northeast's competitiveness must guarantee that the Northeast remains a pleasant and affordable place to live and do business.

Past growth trends present a cautionary tale for future development. Between 1983 and 1997, the amount of urbanized land in the region expanded by 39 percent, while the region's population increased by only seven percent; the result was a 23 percent decrease in overall density. As described in Chapter 2, assuming that the development patterns and polices that guided these trends are left unchanged, between 2000 and 2050 the Northeast's population is projected to increase by 40 percent, while urbanized land will expand by 154 percent. These 40,339 additional square miles of developed land will account for 16 percent of the total land area of the megaregion, an area roughly equivalent to the land area of Virginia.

To meet the challenges of overburdened infrastructure systems, threatened environmental resources, and unrestrained growth trends, strategies will be required that recognize the megaregion is a new phenomenon that crosses state lines and includes cities, suburbs, and rural areas as well as many separate metropolitan regions. To succeed, these efforts will require civic leaders, public officials, and community members to work toward a set of common goals. More importantly, there must be a clear rationale for cooperation across the whole megaregion, one that transcends traditional local and metropolitan-level planning. The solutions to these megaregional problems must be consistent with their size and scope and provide benefits across all the Northeast's metropolitan areas.

THE "HOT-COLD" PROBLEM AND THE NEED FOR SYNERGY ACROSS THE REGION

As part of the study of the Northeast region conducted at the University of Pennsylvania in 2005, data were collected on the median rent, percent of individuals below poverty, and percent of individuals 25 and older with advanced degrees; the information was organized by zip code from the 2000 Census. Employment statistics between 1994 and 2000 were added in each zip code from Zip Code Business Patterns. Each indicator in each zip code was given a ranking from 1, indicating a "hot" area mapped in red, to 10, indicating a "cold" area, mapped in blue. An average of all four categories was taken to give shades of red to hotter areas with low numbers and shades of blue to colder areas with high numbers. The resulting map is Figure 6-2.

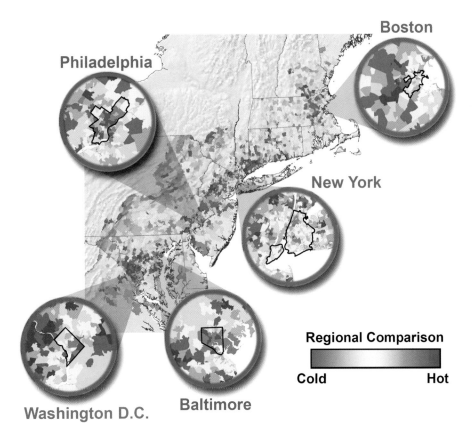

Fig. 6-2: "Hot-Cold" map shows the patterns of new investment in areas within the Northeast Megalopolis.

The map shows newly urbanized areas concentrated in former suburbs to have the largest number of "hot" temperatures, while cities and many rural areas are colder. Of the region's five major cities, New York, Boston, and the west side of Washington register as least cold, while

Baltimore and Philadelphia still show cold economies, despite the resurgence of their downtown districts. A number of the megaregion's second-tier cities, such as Springfield, Massachusetts; Hartford and Bridgeport, Connecticut; Paterson and Camden, New Jersey; and Scranton, Pennsylvania, register as "cold" economies. One conclusion: While "hot" cities and suburban regions like New York, Washington, and Boston are suffering from increasing congestion and rising housing prices, "cold" cities like Philadelphia and Baltimore have both the capacity and the political will to accommodate additional growth.

A smart growth alternative would be to attract a larger share of the Northeast's new development to "cold" areas, through improved transportation links between "hot" and "cold" places and targeted investments in quality of life, housing, education, and other activities in "cold" areas. These new investments could provide underperforming areas with an opportunity to develop underused land, improve access to jobs, and provide affordable housing. Not only will these improvements help turn "colder" areas warm, but they will also relieve the pressure on "hotter" areas of the region where additional growth may compromise future efficiency, attractiveness, and livability.

Improving inter-city transportation emerges as the most obvious first step to improving the physical connections between metropolitan areas, and a step that benefits the economy, growth patterns, and environmental quality in the region.

REGIONAL TRANSPORTATION
AND GLOBAL COMPETITIVENESS

The Northeast has America's oldest transportation infrastructure and one that is truly inter-modal. In addition to the interstate highway system, bus transit, freight railways, and airports also found in other metropolitan areas, there is extensive passenger rail service along Amtrak's Northeast corridor and well-established commuter and local rail transit systems in the Boston, New York, Philadelphia, and Washington areas—as well as a less complete rail transit system in Baltimore and five other cities within the region. Congestion plagues the region's highways, airports, and seaports, whose capacity has been largely used up, while decades of underfunding and disinvestment have greatly reduced the effectiveness of most of the rail transit systems. However, the Northeast has an advantage: Many of its existing land-use patterns were formed in the railroad, subway, and streetcar age.

Strategic investments in the transportation network could redirect growth to reinforce existing development, rather than continue the current pattern of decentralization and reduced population density. Such investments could strengthen the Northeast's economic prospects, provide important environmental benefits, and improve the region's quality of life. The transformation of the Northeast's transportation system into a more effective multi-modal network could alleviate highway congestion, increase transit ridership, speed goods movement, and improve the efficiency of transportation operations throughout the region.

Many of the Northeast's economic competitors in European and Asian megaregions are investing in new multi-modal transportation systems. At the heart of these systems are new high-speed rail networks, providing fast inter-city connections for trips between 100 and 400 miles. High-speed rail can integrate formerly separate metropolitan economies and promote new development in formerly "cold" places. High-speed rail can also reduce commuter congestion on highways and particularly at airports, as noted previously, providing a broad range of economic and mobility benefits. The key to the success of these systems is their integration with other modes of transportation, including airports, urban rail transit, and highways, as well as with urban development, such as the clustering of major employment centers around high-speed rail stations.

The Acela service offered by Amtrak between Washington and Boston has improved travel times along the route, but it is not a high-speed service like the ones offered in Europe or Japan. Creating a truly high-speed rail system in the Northeast will be difficult, expensive, and time consuming, since the urban core of the region is largely built-out, and there are no existing suitable rights-of-way that could be adapted to this purpose. While options for building and financing such a system are analyzed, the smart growth alternative would be continued improvements in speed, frequency, and reliability for the Northeast's existing Amtrak Northeast Corridor inter-city rail system. If the federal government persists in its efforts to dismantle Amtrak, it may be necessary for leaders in the Northeast region to create a new regional entity to manage this system. This action could provide the impetus for a new level of cooperation among the Northeastern states.

Improving Amtrak's Northeast Corridor's level of service, performance, and management could attract new riders who do not currently travel by rail, thus alleviating congestion by taking cars off highways, and in particular, the Northeast's "Main Street": Interstate-95. Intelligent transportation systems and transportation demand management strategies could also reduce congestion on I-95 and the region's other overburdened, limited-access highways. Improved usability and reliability of the highway network, for both passengers and freight movements, would improve the region's livability and create the right capacity for population and economic growth.

TIME IS RUNNING OUT FOR THE
REGION'S ENVIRONMENTAL ASSETS

Drinking water for 55 million people in the Northeast comes from watersheds that are vulnerable to urbanization. The Delaware River watershed, which provides water to 15 million people in the New York City and Philadelphia regions, is threatened by contaminants associated with urbanization and continued development pressures. The Housatonic River, flowing through western Massachusetts and Connecticut, near Bridgeport and New Haven, has some of the highest concentrations of polychlorinated biphenyls in the nation. Water pollution has already decimated Chesapeake Bay's extensive shellfish and blue crab fisheries, and worse damage to the bay is threatened by the urbanization of the Susquehanna River watershed, where impervious surfaces increased by 250,000 acres between 1990 and 2000. The Chesapeake's valuable sports fishery and recreational boating industries are now threatened by diminished water quality.

Rapid urbanization that relies on highway and road access has consumed tens of millions of acres of open land across the Northeast. Recent land consumption rates throughout the 14 states range from 0.38 acres per person in Maryland, which has strong smart growth policies, to a staggering 3.16 acres per person in Pennsylvania.

Large swaths of the region's most significant and sensitive ecological and recreational zones lie in the direct path of projected development to 2025 and 2050. If current development trends and policies continue, the whole Northeast region will become a continuous band of urban development within a few decades.

This urbanization forecast for the Northeast region is based on Woods and Poole population forecasts by county to 2025, which were then projected out to 2050. These population projections were then related to land consumption rates per person in each state, based on the trends between 1982 and 1997. Using the Spatial Analyst program in ArcView GIS, a raster field map was created composed of 100-acre cells. Each cell was assigned an impedance value linked to the presence of existing urbanization, bodies of water, federally or state protected land, and proximity to existing centers and transportation infrastructure. Cells were recognized by the computer program as growth areas in accordance with their impedance value and the acres of land consumption projected for each county for 2025 and 2050. Where a county was shown as becoming built out in either projection period, projected urbanization was shifted to adjacent counties. However, state lines were always respected, and growth projections from one state were not added to the projections in another state, as the land consumption statistics are particular to each state.

Figure 6-3 shows the large natural open-space systems in the Northeast region as compiled by the Appalachian Mountain Club. A second

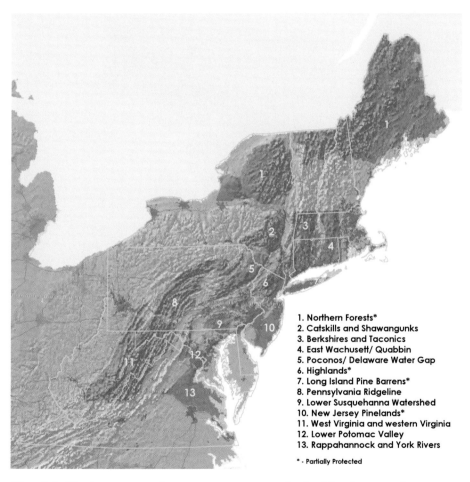

1. Northern Forests*
2. Catskills and Shawangunks
3. Berkshires and Taconics
4. East Wachusett/ Quabbin
5. Poconos/ Delaware Water Gap
6. Highlands*
7. Long Island Pine Barrens*
8. Pennsylvania Ridgeline
9. Lower Susquehanna Watershed
10. New Jersey Pinelands*
11. West Virginia and western Virginia
12. Lower Potomac Valley
13. Rappahannock and York Rivers

* - Partially Protected

Fig. 6-3: The large natural open-space systems in the Northeast region as compiled by the Appalachian Mountain Club.

map [Figure 6-4] shows the results of urbanization projections to 2025 and 2050 and illustrates how the existing patterns of urbanization, if they continue, are likely to consume much of the region's natural open space.

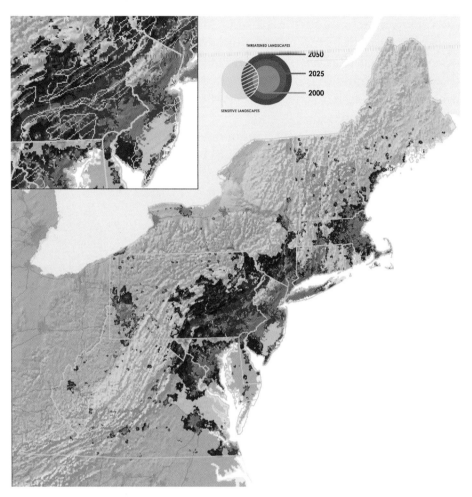

Fig. 6-4: Urbanization projections to 2025 and 2050 illustrate how the existing growth patterns, if they continue, are likely to consume much of the region's natural open space.

Preserving the Northeast's large natural resource systems and open spaces would provide important economic as well as environmental and public health benefits. The region's quality of life—in part underpinned by the existence and accessibility of these resources—helps attract and retain the region's advanced technology and service industries and their skilled workers. The natural systems also represent a green infra-structure, providing stormwater management, natural purification of water, and natural absorption and elimination of air pollutants.

The protection of the Northeast's green infrastructure can be a vital shaping component of a growth management strategy for the entire Northeast region. A variety of regulatory tools are available for pro-tecting open space, include zoning, establishing protected areas, chang-ing development guidelines, and creating urban growth boundaries, all of which can be used to promote more compact, less land-consuming patterns of development. The Northeast has already demonstrated suc-cess in protecting important landscapes and resource systems through the creation of regional land-use regulatory agencies, in such places as the Adirondack Park, the New Jersey Pinelands, Cape Cod, Martha's Vineyard, the Long Island Pine Barrens, and most recently, in the New Jersey Highlands.

Incentive-based tools such as tax breaks, purchase of conservation easements, and transfer of development rights programs are also tools at hand. TDR programs, when implemented at the regional scale, as in the New Jersey Pinelands, may prove effective in preserving sensitive landscapes and directing growth toward existing urban areas.

BYPASSED LAND: THE NEXT URBAN FRONTIER

Although the phenomenon varies among the region's metropolitan areas, cities and suburbs throughout the Northeast are burdened with underused parcels, ranging from urban "gap" sites to former industrial areas, as well as underused strips of commercial land along suburban arterial highways and the sites of closed or dying shopping malls. Across the Northeast region, suburban greenfield sites are being con-sumed for development instead of these abundant infill and redevelop-ment opportunities, requiring new investments in infrastructure and further weakening "cold" urban and suburban areas where the neces-sary infrastructure for development is already in place. On average, 10 percent of the land area of cities in the Northeast region, totaling almost 2,000 square miles,[4] is vacant. At an average density of six dwelling units per acre, offering a variety of community options from high urban den-sity to single-family dwellings, infill development could accommodate over seven million households, or 77 percent of the region's projected growth to 2050. Promoting infill development makes better use of exist-ing infrastructure and offers an important opportunity to both boost the growth of "cold" areas and ease the high cost of living and doing business in nearby "hot" ones.

The Northeast region contains 10 cities with rail transit systems, ranging from the extensive metropolitan New York system (with 962 stations) to Lancaster, Pennsylvania's new system (with three planned stations). Almost half of the potential infill development sites in the Northeast are within half a mile of existing or planned fixed route tran sit. Policies should encourage development within walking distance of transit. The creation of a network of origins and destinations along the transit system could help to revitalize existing communities and increase the use of transit systems while creating a framework for compact, walkable, mixed use development throughout the region. This form of development will be particularly suitable for the region's expected demographic shift towards larger concentrations of the elderly, immigrants, and younger singles, all of whom are likely to prefer more compact, transit-oriented housing and communities.

The map [Figure 6-5] shows how the projected population growth and development trends in the megaregion could be directed away from greenfield areas towards locations supported by transit and where infill development is possible.

The redirection of growth towards vacant land within already urbanized areas complements the goals of protecting the Northeast's green infrastructure and strengthening the transportation system and intercity connections. Barriers to infill development, such as the additional cost of redeveloping brownfield sites, need to be mitigated by techniques to shield developers from liability and assist in environmental remediation costs. Successful models across the country, such as land banks that facilitate the preparation of parcels, can speed the development of brownfields. For example, Atlanta's Fulton County Land Bank Authority undertakes the inventory, organization, and preparation of these parcels for transfer to private developers. Other authorities, such as the Louisville Metro Land Bank, are not only empowered to clear titles, but also to acquire and remediate brownfield properties, further lowering the cost to the private market and spurring redevelopment. These authorities are then capable of marketing the newly prepared parcels and promoting well-coordinated development through comprehensive plans and tax policies.

Ideally, a functional infill development program would begin at the metropolitan level while maintaining a regional perspective. In the United

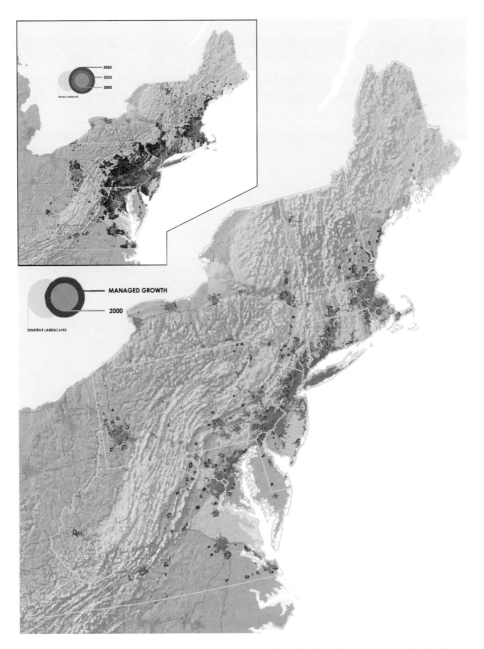

Fig. 6-5: All the projected population growth and development trends in the megaregion could be accommodated in locations supported by transit where infill development is possible. The inset shows Figure 6-4 [page 86] for comparison.

Kingdom, beginning with the construction of a national land-use database in 1998, the central government has employed its exclusive development permitting powers to implement a national policy that promotes infill redevelopment. While there is no equivalent planning authority in the U.S., a consortium of state and metropolitan planning agencies or city planning commissions, in coordination with a broader strategy for the whole Northeast region, could create incentives or regulatory reforms to promote infill, perhaps coupled with a broader transfer-of-development rights program designed to move development out of designated conservation areas. This diagram [Figure 6-6] describes the mix of public policies needed for a balanced and equitable future for the Northeast Megaregion.

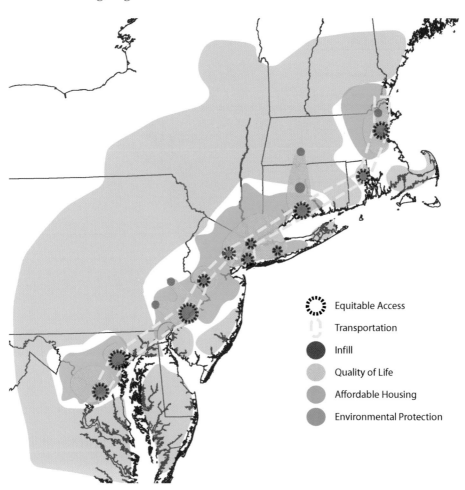

Fig. 6-6: This diagram outlines the public policies recommended for the Northeast Megaregion.

THE NEED FOR NEW KINDS OF INSTITUTIONS

To create an integrated multi-modal transportation system, redirect growth from "hot" to "cold" areas, and achieve effective environmental conservation, the Northeast region, with a land area comparable to the state of California, must contend with an exceptionally fragmented governance system, encompassing 11 states and the District of Columbia, 405 counties, several thousand cities and towns, and an even larger number of special service and tax districts. To achieve regional goals, some kind of new governance framework is needed in which political, civic, and business leaders can work together. This framework could take several shapes, ranging from federal incentives for increased regional cooperation; to a bottom-up, civic, or business-led initiative; or a middle ground in which states and regions form voluntary partnerships around specific issues, perhaps encouraged by federal incentives.

Civic and business-led regional planning has a good track record in the Northeast and may be the most appropriate starting place in light of limited current federal interest in national planning initiatives. The region has a long tradition of civic leadership on important public issues and the nation's most extensive network of non-governmental organizations. Civic groups in the Northeast have long led planning efforts at the regional scale:

• In the 1920s, the Massachusetts Trustees of Reservations proposed creation of The Bay Circuit, a permanent greenbelt to shape metropolitan Boston's growth.

• The 1929 *Regional Plan for New York and its Environs*, which laid the groundwork for the highways, bridges, transit systems, and parks that shaped the New York-New Jersey-Connecticut region, was spearheaded by the Regional Plan Association, a group of civic and business leaders inspired by the challenge of accommodating the long-term growth of the New York metropolitan area. Today, RPA is spearheading the America 2050 initiative in cooperation with the Lincoln Institute of Land Policy.

• In watersheds and important natural resource areas, from the Adirondacks and North Woods of Maine, Vermont, and New Hampshire to Long Island Sound and the Chesapeake Bay, regional environmental groups are leading public education and advocacy campaigns in support of efforts to protect these landscapes.

Comparable civic advocacy at the megaregion scale could provide the impetus for tackling the challenges facing the Northeast. RPA has initiated a process of discussions with government, business, academic, and civic stakeholders to reach agreement on a set of strategies and priority investments for the Northeast, complemented by a public education campaign to foster an understanding of the threats and opportunities facing the region.

To gain momentum and a sense of urgency for these discussions, coalitions should be formed around current issues with an immediate impact on the entire region. The current crisis in Amtrak funding could create the impetus for such a coalition, with the goal of achieving real reform of Northeast corridor rail service. Revitalization of Amtrak into a truly effective transportation system could create the setting for a major expansion of urban transit and inter-city rail throughout the Northeast.

The role of the natural environment as green infrastructure could be a strong impetus for environmental conservation. New York City's experience in protecting its upstate reservoirs from the pollution caused by development could be a good example. It proved far more cost-effective to conserve the natural environment than to build the water-treatment facilities that would have been needed to treat the contamination caused by development.[5]

When the state of Maryland made a serious comparison between the long-term costs of providing transportation, infrastructure, and municipal services to greenfield sites, as opposed to financing infill development in areas that already have the services, transportation, and infrastructure they need, administrators and legislators concluded that the state could not afford to continue policies that encourage low-density development at the edge of its metropolitan areas. Maryland's smart growth policies could be a model for other states in the region.

NOTES

1. Portions of this chapter are excerpted and adapted from the final report of a graduate planning studio at the University of Pennsylvania in the spring of 2005, *Reinventing Megalopolis: The Northeast Megaregion* (University of Pennsylvania School of Design, Spring 2005), directed by Robert D. Yaro and Armando Carbonell. The student participants were Tony Cho, Martine Combal, Mary DiCarlantonio, Geraldine Gooding, Doug Giuliano, Masaru Iwakawa, David Kooris, Mara Marino, Heather McCall, Nash Mewborn, Emily Moos, Taylor Pankonien, Tyler Patrick, Amy Pettine, Megan Ritchie, and Jessica Tump.

The research results were also shaped by a week-long workshop held at the Fundación Metrópoli in Madrid, Spain, in March 2005. At this workshop, the Penn studio worked with a distinguished group of European scholars and practitioners in European spatial planning. The workshop also included a team of graduate students from Georgia Tech, led by Catherine Ross and Cheryl Contant, who were participating in a parallel studio on the Southeast Piedmont Megalopolis.

The studio was also advised by a panel of prominent business, civic, and government leaders from Massachusetts, Rhode Island, New York, Pennsylvania, Maryland, and the District of Columbia. The studio's final presentation was to this group and 10 state planning directors from Northeastern states, convened by the Lincoln Institute of Land Policy and Regional Plan Association. This group identified a set of key actions on which the Northeastern states could collaborate to begin to shape the megaregion's future growth and development.

2. Jean Gottmann, *Megalopolis: The Urbanized Northeastern Seaboard of the United States*, Cambridge, Mass.: M.I.T. Press, 1961.

3. Regional Plan Association, "The Region's Growth," New York: 1967.

4. Michael A. Pagano and Ann O'M. Bowman, "Vacant Land in Cities: an Urban Resource," Washington, D.C.: Brookings Institution, December 2000.

5. Winnie Hu, "Striving to Protect the Watershed, the City Assumes the Role of Country Land Baron," *The New York Times*, August 9, 2004: p. B1.

7

Natural Hazards and Regional Design[1]

Jonathan Barnett

In *Design with Nature,* published in 1969, Ian McHarg told architects and landscape architects that they should emulate the economical way in which nature resolves conflicting forces and incorporate nature itself in their design. Designers who failed to take this advice could expect to be punished by future events. Build a house on a dune overlooking the ocean, and the ocean may very well wash both dune and house away. The house destabilizes the natural balance of the dune; the new natural balance does not include the house; and the dune reforms farther back from the water. The house belongs on the land behind the dune, in harmony with the natural balance of the sea shore.

In the late 1960s, when Ian McHarg was writing *Design with Nature,* the climate of the entire planet, which had been relatively stable for some 11,000 years, was beginning to change because of carbon and other chemicals issuing from factory smokestacks and from vehicle exhaust pipes. These pollutants trap the sun's energy and produce "the greenhouse effect"—a rise in temperature in the earth's atmosphere. It took time for scientists to be sure that a permanent change in the world's climate has occurred, not just normal fluctuations that can be expected from year to year. Today, scientific opinion is close to unanimous that the world's temperature is getting warmer. The potential changes are so big that we are no longer talking only about whether a house is in the wrong place along a shore, but about whether whole cities and regions are in danger.

SAVING OUR CITIES AND REGIONS FROM CLIMATE CHANGE

Scientists disagree about how much warmer the planet has already become and how fast the global temperature is rising, but many think it is already too late to stop some further change. Global warming causes the sea level to rise. Part of the rise comes from the expansion of the water itself, which occupies more space as it becomes warmer. Part of the change is from melting snow and ice washing off mountain peaks and the Arctic and Antarctic ice caps. Polar ice seems to be melting faster than anyone expected a few years ago. Melting ice that is already resting in the sea will not raise water levels, but melting ice from snow and glaciers on land will pour water into the sea.

Warmer sea water also intensifies storms. Scientists say we can expect more hurricanes like Katrina, the powerful storm that hit the U.S. Gulf coast in 2005. Warming air temperatures also change the way air currents move around the world. One result can be drought. Some places, like the southern Mediterranean area and Southwest Australia, are receiving less rain than they used to, and this change could be permanent.

A very conservative estimate of the rise in sea levels already in progress and impossible to reverse is one-third of a meter (over a foot) by the year 2050 and a full meter (over three feet) by 2100. These are worldwide averages, so sea level rise could be greater in some places and less in others. Rising water levels exaggerate the effects of unusual conditions: High tides are higher; storm surges are more powerful and cover a larger land area. Cities and regions in low-lying areas will have to make big changes to deal with these new conditions. One of the areas most at risk is the Netherlands, where much of the land in the Rhine River delta is already below sea level. Scientists and planners are looking at a new design for the entire country of the Netherlands, seeking areas where some intrusion of water could be accepted, rather than relying on dykes to keep sea water out completely.

ACHIEVING A NEW GLOBAL EQUILIBRIUM

In the hundreds of thousands of years that human beings have existed, the evidence from archaeology is that only in about the last 10,000 years have people been able to create complex societies and build on the achievements of past generations. Many scientists have concluded that it has been the relatively mild and stable world climate during these years that has permitted civilization to develop. Today civilization has become so dependent on modern machinery and social institutions that it is easily disrupted. The fragility of modern urbanized life is one reason to be concerned about the changes now beginning to take place in the earth's temperature. If nations do not unite and take strong measures to slow down the progress of climate change, in the next century we are likely to enter a period where global temperatures are much higher than they have been before in recorded history. The population of the globe will also be larger than it is now, so that resources will be scarcer and more people are likely to be living in areas that are vulnerable to change. Human beings are remaking the planet, and it is a dangerous experiment. The prudent course is to try to prevent as much climate change as possible.

The world needs to find substitutes for coal, oil, and natural gas, as burning them for energy is a prime cause of global climate change. While this search for effective energy substitutes is going on, designers can help by creating environments that need less energy or natural resources to sustain them.

CONSERVE THE NATURAL ENVIRONMENT

The natural environment is like a design, in that it represents the resolution of conflicting forces. Once the landscape is destabilized by development, it can take a long time for natural systems to reach a new equilibrium, and this new environment is likely to be far less desirable for people than it was before. Many of the problems with soil erosion and flooding are traceable to poorly planned development. Leaving the landscape undisturbed, or in well-managed agricultural use, is the best way to protect against erosion and flooding.

Regional development should be looked at as a design problem. The areas of sensitive natural ecology, which, as Ian McHarg suggested, could be destabilized by new construction, should be mapped as protected before planning begins. Highways and transit lines in newly developing areas should be planned so that they support a series of compact, mixed use communities—and stay well clear of areas that should be protected.

LESSONS FROM HURRICANE KATRINA

Hurricane Katrina struck New Orleans on August 29, 2005. Flood walls and levees failed in multiple locations the next day, leaving much of the city uninhabitable. Less than a month later, on September 23 and 24, rain from Hurricane Rita overwhelmed temporary patches in the flood protection structures, re-flooded areas that had been pumped dry, and made things even worse in the large areas where the city was still inundated. After the hurricanes, some argued that New Orleans ought to be rebuilt on a "smaller footprint," limiting rebuilding to those areas that were not flooded after Katrina.

That argument avoids the most important question of all: Why should the city have flooded in the first place? Just before hitting land, Katrina veered 30 miles to the east and diminished to a Category 3 storm. The levees and flood walls that failed in New Orleans were supposed to handle such a storm; the U.S. Army Corps of Engineers later acknowledged that the disaster was caused by design and construction failures. Using these accidental flood patterns as an excuse to downsize the city would be unfair to the residents who had already suffered devastating damages, and defeatist for an economic comeback.

For now it has been agreed that flood protection for New Orleans will be rebuilt at least at the level originally intended (a Category 3 storm), flood gates along waterways will be added, and vulnerabilities, like the inland location of pumps, will be corrected. New Orleans will be replanned on the assumption that it can and will return to its former size, accepting that recovery will be slow for the most devastated parts of the city. [Figure 7-1]

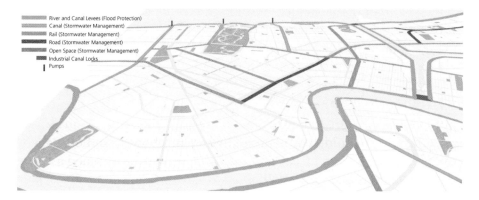

Fig. 7-1: This diagram shows the location of new or repaired flood walls and levees needed in New Orleans plus the locations for relocating pumps at the perimeter of the city. A century ago, the facilities were at the city perimeter; now they are deep within populated areas.

These decisions do not answer the criticisms of those who argue that the city should not be rebuilt at all. They ask what would have happened if the storm had not swerved to the east and if the winds had not diminished. Parts of the city of New Orleans are below sea level, but the historic central area is not. However, the entire city is below the level of the adjacent Mississippi River, which is controlled by an artificial channel. Some experts think that flooding from the Mississippi is New Orleans's biggest long-term problem (one it shares with Baton Rouge, where many people and businesses have relocated). A direct hit on New Orleans by a Category 5 storm would almost certainly have overtopped and possibly breached the Mississippi levees that survived Katrina. The whole of New Orleans is likely to have flooded, including the Super Bowl stadium that was used as an evacuation center after Katrina.

Global climate change is believed to be making hurricanes stronger and more frequent. If that is true, then New Orleans's only reliable protection from all potential floods and storm surges would combine the prevention measures already being put in place with restoration of a protective band of wetlands along the whole Mississippi delta—including modifications to the Mississippi River channel. Such a project would take decades and would require the participation of three states and the federal government. In the meantime, New Orleans remains the only city along the Gulf Coast that has any significant hurricane protection, except for the seawall at Galveston, where some 8,000 people were killed in 1900 by a storm surge of more than 15 feet that swept across the entire Galveston Island.

On September 2, 2005, immediately after Katrina, Rep. Dennis Hastert, Speaker of the U.S. House of Representatives, was reported as saying this: "It makes no sense to spend billions of dollars to rebuild a city that's seven feet under sea level." He then went on to add: "But you know we build Los Angeles and San Francisco on top of earthquake fissures and they rebuild, too." After indignant reactions from Louisiana's governor and congressional representatives, Rep. Hastert issued a statement saying he was not "advocating that New Orleans be abandoned or relocated. My comments about rebuilding the city were intended to reflect my sincere concern with how the city is rebuilt to ensure the future protection of its citizens and not to suggest that this great and historic city should not be rebuilt."

The Speaker opened the door to an important discussion, and then hastily closed it again. The rationale for spending billions of federal dollars on rebuilding and protecting New Orleans is that the city relied on a federal agency, the U.S. Army Corps of Engineers, for protection, and that protection failed in storm conditions that were supposed to be within its capacity. These circumstances have pushed aside any meaningful consideration during the reconstruction effort of the city's continued vulnerability, dysfunctional governance, and shrinking economic base. New Orleans is an important part of the U.S. cultural and architectural heritage, a leading tourist destination and convention location, a regional business center, the home of a university of national importance (Tulane) and several significant local ones. It is also part of the world's fourth or fifth largest port by tonnage—although not in numbers of containers, the more usual measure. All the same, the city remains in an exposed location, and unless a regional protection system is created for the Gulf Coast, a worse disaster is still a possibility.

RISK FROM NATURAL HAZARDS IS A NATIONAL PROBLEM

Speaker Hastert was right to raise questions about the costs of protecting New Orleans while also mentioning the earthquake threat to Los Angeles and San Francisco. The only equitable way to discuss this subject is in the context of the vulnerabilities of all U.S. cities. New Orleans and the Gulf Coast are not the only parts of the U.S. facing flood surges produced by tropical storms. The storm evacuation maps displayed on an official New York City website show that a direct hit by a Category 3 hurricane will produce a flood surge—depending on the tides—of up to 30 feet. This surge could extend across Manhattan Island beyond Canal Street and impact most of the city's shoreline, inundating both Kennedy and LaGuardia airports. Even a Category 1 storm will produce some flooding. [Figure 7-2]

Destruction would go beyond buildings at street level. Most of New York City's subway lines converge in Lower Manhattan, and water from a storm surge would flow down open subway stairs and through street ventilation grates. Many of the ventilation shafts for the Brooklyn Battery, Holland, Lincoln, and Queens Midtown Tunnels are in or near the rivers and likewise appear to be vulnerable to a flood surge. So, too, are the Amtrak and the Long Island Railroad river-tunnels. A year after Katrina, 40 percent of New Orleans was without electricity. How long would it take to repair New York City's subways and other underground infrastructure? What would the city be like in the meantime?

Fig. 7-2: A diagram prepared from hurricane evacuation maps on an official New York City website. A direct hit by even a Category 1 (orange) storm could cause a flood surge that would inundate large land areas and flow down into train and vehicular tunnels. Damage from a Category 2 (yellow) or 3 (green) storm would extend even farther.

The configuration of New York Harbor makes Jamaica Bay, lower Manhattan, and the East and Hudson riverfronts especially vulnerable to a devastating combination of winds and tides, but the odds of such a catastrophe afflicting New York City appear to be lower than the recurrence of a major hurricane in New Orleans. Hurricane Betsy in 1965 created a flood surge in low-lying wards of New Orleans similar to the surge from Hurricane Katrina, although not as severe. The last time lower Manhattan was hit by a flood surge from a hurricane was in the early 19th century, and the storm hit at low tide, which minimized the damage. Some people think that the route followed by Hurricane Carol in 1954 had the potential for catastrophic destruction in New York City, but Carol was a relatively small storm and it turned out to be a near miss, veering east and striking Long Island and the Connecticut shore instead. Destructive storm surges from direct hurricane hits are also possible in other major coastal cities such as Baltimore, Philadelphia, and Boston. Consider the 1938 hurricane that devastated the eastern end of Long Island then made a direct hit on the Connecticut and Rhode Island shore. The storm surge in downtown Providence was 15 to 20 feet deep.

None of the cities on the East Coast has any storm-surge protection, nor do Gulf Coast cities like Corpus Christi or Pensacola. The entire state of Florida is vulnerable to hurricanes from both the Atlantic Ocean and the Gulf of Mexico. Rising ocean levels make storm surges more likely, particularly in south Florida, where the land elevations are low. Miami and Miami Beach are both close to sea level. If a one-foot rise in worldwide sea level does materialize by 2050, those two cities and many others will be more vulnerable to storm surges. If no protections are instituted, parts of some cities could be under water even on a normal day. [Figure 7-3]

For much of our nation's history, it has seemed reasonable to say that if a beach erodes in a storm, the previous shoreline should be restored. However, if in fact there is a dynamic situation where sea levels are steadily rising, then the decision to build, and rebuild, in eroding shore areas may no longer make sense. As Rob Evans of the Woods Hole Ocean and Climate Change Institute put it: "There is a price for living at sea level and building upon sand." The one-foot rise in sea level predicted by 2050 raises risks because high tide comes farther up the shore and the effect of a storm tide becomes that much more severe. A one meter rise in sea level predicted by 2100 will change some shorelines completely. [Figure 7-4, page 104]

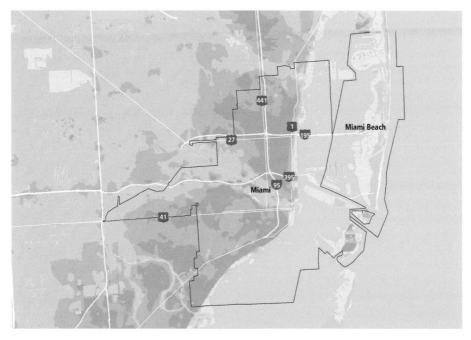

Fig. 7-3: These two maps show Miami and Miami Beach today, and then the effect of a hypothetical one-foot rise in sea level, predicted as possible by 2050. Flood protection measures would make the Miami area's relation to the sea more like that of New Orleans.

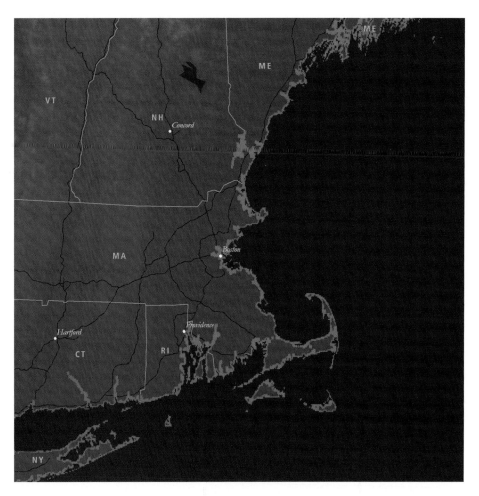

Fig. 7-4: A map of the northeastern U.S. showing the effect of a hypothetical one-meter rise in sea level predicted as possible by 2100. Many shoreline properties would be affected, as would cities like Boston and Providence.

OTHER URBAN AREAS AT RISK

Earthquakes are less predictable than hurricanes but also unavoidable. San Francisco and Los Angeles are obviously vulnerable, but so also are all the other West Coast cities near the Pacific Ocean. What were probably the largest earthquakes in U.S. history did not occur on the West Coast, however. In 1811 and 1812, there were three great shocks along the New Madrid Fault in Arkansas, Missouri, Kentucky, and Tennessee, an area then largely uninhabited. The quakes caused the Mississippi

River to take a new course and are said to have made church bells ring as far away as Charleston, South Carolina. Today Memphis is the major city most likely to be seriously affected by a recurrence. St. Louis would be affected also. Salt Lake City and other population centers along the Wasatch Fault are likewise at risk. Charleston suffered a major earthquake in 1886, and Boston in 1775.

Droughts and accompanying wildfires may become more frequent and of longer duration as the result of climate change. A recent op-ed piece in the New York Times by Roger Kennedy, a former director of the National Park Service, states that "half of the nation's population growth is taking place in the 10 fastest growing states; seven of these states rank in the top 10 in the percentage of their population at risk from wildfire." Kennedy's prescription is a "National Flame Zone Atlas" that would inform home buyers of potential risk and tell governments where not to encourage development.

As noted in Chapter 2, the U.S. population is likely to increase by 50 percent by 2050, with much of the growth predicted for multi-city regions where earthquakes are possible, to coastlines subject to storm surges and changes in sea level, or to areas where there is a risk of wildfire. A first step would be to generalize from Roger Kennedy's advice and make a serious national effort to catalogue the geographic extent of potential disaster areas and the probabilities that such disasters may actually happen. This information could inform local governments' decisions about zoning codes and other development regulations, and would be useful to insurance companies, investors, and home buyers. The reason for making such a catalogue a national effort is fairness: All property owners should know about the risks in every location.

GUARDING AGAINST SYSTEMIC FAILURE OF WHOLE CITIES

San Francisco after the earthquake and fire in 1906, Galveston after the hurricane of 1900, and New Orleans after Katrina are examples of destruction so complete that an entire city ceases to function. New York City, if it were hit by the kind of flood surge portrayed on its official website, might well suffer systemic failure, as so much of its basic transportation infrastructure would flood. Miami Beach and Miami are at risk of widespread damage from a flood surge. San Francisco and Los Angeles are relatively well-prepared for an earthquake, but other cities with a similar degree of risk are not. Much of Boston is built on filled land. Although seismic codes were introduced in the early 1970s, most buildings in Boston, including many historic structures and most of the utilities, do not have modern earthquake protection. The Salt Lake City, the Pacific Northwest, and the Memphis regions are other places with earthquake hazards but little in the way of comprehensive protection against building and utility failures.

When we look at the level of disaster preparedness in New Orleans and the deficiencies in the response of the federal government after Katrina, it is unclear how well the U.S. economy could recover from comparable events in other major cities, particularly if several happened within a few years of each other. The potential damage from a cluster of disasters suggests that this is a homeland security issue, and that national expenditures for protection and preparedness would be the prudent public policy. In flood-prone cities, levees and flood gates could be installed, particularly protection for transit and vehicle tunnels. In earthquake-prone cities, programs that would help owners retrofit buildings for seismic protection as well as strong building codes for new buildings and programs to retrofit utilities, would be good long-term investments.

Since urbanization is no longer constrained by the location considerations that prevailed in previous centuries, it would be possible to direct expected increases in population growth away from areas at risk from flood surges or earthquakes towards relatively safe places. The U.S. Constitution is considered to have left planning issues to the states, but national planning for disaster preparedness is a legitimate federal issue, like coastal zone management. In all the conversations about smart growth, little is said about not building in harm's way. It is time to add such considerations to decisions about future development.

NOTE

1. Portions of this chapter appeared in the *Wharton Real Estate Review*, fall 2006.

8

Smart Growth in Cities and Towns

Jonathan Barnett[1]

The architect for a proposed Wal-Mart in Omaha, Nebraska, was asked at a public hearing why his building looked so much less appealing than a Wal-Mart in Fort Collins, Colorado. His reply struck a nerve: "Fort Collins has design guidelines, and you don't." Omaha's political and business leaders had been committed for years to improving downtown. Now they became aware that the image of the city could be shaped by decisions about prominent sites along peripheral highways. They then decided that Omaha needed design guidelines, not just for big box stores but for the entire city.

How do you write design guidelines for a whole city? The state and federal constitutions limit what a local government can do about private property. Local zoning and subdivision regulations are the basic tools for managing growth, and what they say about design not only relates to constitutional limits, but also to what is acceptable to business leaders, developers, and the public.

Reaching agreement on design issues for a whole city or town is not the same as creating guidelines for a historic district, which only need to define the essence of what should be preserved. Devising guidelines for a Wal-Mart or other suburban retail structure in a parking lot, surrounded by other retail buildings in their parking lots, is not like the more familiar task of writing guidelines for closely spaced buildings on downtown streets. Fort Collins does indeed have regulations for the massing and facades of big retail buildings, but the problem is also the location of the building, how it relates to the street, to the topography, and to other buildings and uses. The subdivisions and strip malls going up on the outskirts of Omaha need to be related to each other and to the surrounding landscape. The development regulations should be as effective as the way developers can control what happens on their individual properties. Unfortunately, many of the most successful examples of designed development are based on sales contracts between the master developer and the buyers of individual property parcels, like the design controls at Battery Park City in Manhattan, or the regulating plans at Seaside, the Kentlands, or other master planned communities that are controlled by a single property owner. Design in these situations is part of a private transaction: If you don't like the design controls, you don't have to buy the parcel. In designing new regulations for a whole city, the community has to agree on what needs to be done and on how to do it. As with a historic district, only at a much larger scale and with a much more varied set of issues, the guidelines must engage the community's beliefs—the design values that everyone can accept. Business leaders and developers also have to agree that the regulations are economically feasible.

UNDERSTANDING OMAHA'S DESIGN CHARACTER

Effective city design always starts with the existing situation, and not with a one-size-fits-all preconception. One of the most important issues is how development relates to the natural landscape. Omaha's early settlers would have found a rolling prairie with meandering creeks along the valleys. Most of the tall trees would have been on or near the creek banks. As they came over the hills, the settlers would have seen a green valley framed by the hills beyond. Today the creeks are in culverts or have been straightened and channeled until they look like little more than drainage-ways. The city's street grid, as in most U.S. cities beyond the Eastern states, was laid out on a mile-square system with little concern for topography. As a result, the underlying landscape is almost forgotten, except when there is a heavy rainstorm and the creeks flood. Creating a better relationship between nature and the built environment in Omaha is not just an aesthetic issue; it is also a question of sustainability and life safety.

Old photographs of downtown Omaha show that it looked much like other traditional U.S. downtowns, except that the streets are steeper than most. Six- and eight-story buildings line the sidewalks, with shops on the ground floor and tenants' advertising signs on the second and even third floor windows and walls. The Old Market district preserves some of this original character, but downtown today is much more open, redeveloped at the scale of the automobile, not the pedestrian. Omaha has a new skyline of tall buildings, a courthouse by Pei Cobb Freed and Partners, an addition to the Joslyn Art Museum by Norman Foster, and a performing arts center by the Polshek Partnership. A few historic buildings survive, and some presentable new ones, plus the usual ration of parking lots and nondescript service structures. The old meat-packing district is gone, replaced by parks. The Gene Leahy Mall, designed by Lawrence Halprin in the 1970s, is a multi-block park with a sunken artificial river that, when the connecting fountain is operating, seems to lead to a surprisingly big lake in the adjacent Heartland of America Park at the edge of the Missouri River. Along the lake is the landscaped campus of Con-Agra, one of five Fortune 500 companies with headquarters in Omaha.

Metropolitan Omaha is growing to the southwest, following expressway connections to Lincoln, the state capital, about 75 miles away, and is part of what will soon be a continuous urbanized area extending from Lincoln to Council Bluffs, Iowa, directly across the Missouri River from Omaha. This urbanized area is, in turn, at the extreme western edge of the Midwest Multi-City Region centered around Chicago. One of the proposed high-speed rail corridors from Chicago would extend to Omaha.

Omaha's downtown corresponds to the core that Ernest W. Burgess would have mapped as the center of five rings of concentric development, but downtown today is only one business center in a chain that stretches westward along Dodge Street 20 miles to the current city limits, to some extent substantiating Homer Hoyt's sector theory of development as well as Harris and Ullman's theory of the city with multiple centers. However, this long east-west corridor, plus five or six north-south business streets that intersect it, does not conform to these early normative theories of how cities develop. It is nevertheless the real downtown for this city of 400,000 within a metropolitan area of 800,000. The developments along these streets form Omaha's front door, the places used by the most people, where having design guidelines is most important.

The older parts of Omaha have traditional neighborhoods with tree-lined streets and local schools, churches, and shops. Many of these neighborhoods are strong and attractive; others show signs of social stress. Much city investment has gone into preserving and improving the poorest neighborhoods; you don't see scenes of inner city devastation. In the rapidly developing newer parts of Omaha, houses and apartments are built in tracts sorted out by sales price or rental category, with few if any trees or other neighborhood amenities. Shopping is located in strip centers. Schools and institutions each have big separate sites. If you want a newly built house, you are unlikely to find one in a traditional neighborhood.

THE DESIGN PROCESS

Creating new development regulations for Omaha involves three sets of design issues: green, civic, and neighborhood. "Green" means relating development to the city's characteristic landscape setting and making the built environment more sustainable. "Civic" means designing desirable and recognizable settings for the parts of the city where most of its business and cultural life takes place. "Neighborhood" means preserving the best qualities of older neighborhoods and seeing these qualities incorporated in new neighborhoods as they develop.

These three sets of issues also correspond to three potential constituencies for urban design: environmentalists, civic or cultural organizations, and neighborhood activists. These groups, as well as urban designers, are working on these issues nationwide. There are many successful examples to draw on. What is unusual is Omaha's effort to deal with design issues across the whole city, reflected in the name given for the effort, Omaha by Design. This comprehensive approach provides a useful summary of the policies and regulations needed by many other U.S. communities.

It took a little over a year for the first phase—agreeing on an urban design element for the Omaha Master Plan—to work its way through the public process and get approved by the Omaha city council. This master plan element focused on what is desirable; the next phase, enacting amendments to Omaha's development regulations and creating other implementation measures, focuses on how to achieve it.

GREEN DESIGN

City design starts with the natural landscape, and in Omaha the most significant landscape element is the creek system and the valleys it has created. In the 1920s, many of the creeks were given straight channels in order to speed flood waters through the system. This is now thought to be precisely the wrong prescription. The regional water district today uses dams to impound waters upstream from the most populated areas, restricting flow until the landscape absorbs the water, or until it is safe to release it. Within the city, development needs to be kept out of the flood plain, which means long-term removal of the remaining buildings that are in the flood plain now. It also means regulations to prevent new development from invading the flood plain, even if the land profile is raised for the new development so that it is technically not in the flood plain any longer. Filling in the flood plain has negative consequences for property owners both upstream and down.

The creek flood plains form what could be a citywide open space system. One of the major urban design initiatives in Omaha, called for in the urban design element of the master plan, is transforming the creeks and their banks into parks. The improvements to Brush Creek in the Country Club Plaza district in Kansas City are being looked at as a prototype. In Kansas City, break-away dams are used to raise the water levels so that Brush Creek is no longer a trickle at the bottom of a steep culvert but a series of narrow lakes. In Omaha, raising the creek levels and improving the immediate surroundings could make adjacent land into waterfront property. [Figures 8-1a and 8-1b, page 112]

GREEN STREETS AND HIGHWAYS

The urban design element of Omaha's master plan calls for more intensive landscaping of the 1,800 acres of highway verges within the city, which are only minimally landscaped today. Highways are opportunities for large-scale landscape compositions that can improve the image of the city at a relatively low cost. [Figures 8-2a and 8-2b, page 113] The urban design element also includes a green streets policy, which is being implemented through the creation of a streetscape handbook. It also turns out that Omaha's subdivision ordinance has no requirements for street trees in low-density residential districts. This omission is being corrected.

GREEN PARKING LOTS

Perhaps the most characteristic image of the modern U.S. city is the parking lot. While it is desirable to hide parking behind buildings, and garages are the better design choice in high-profile civic areas, today's

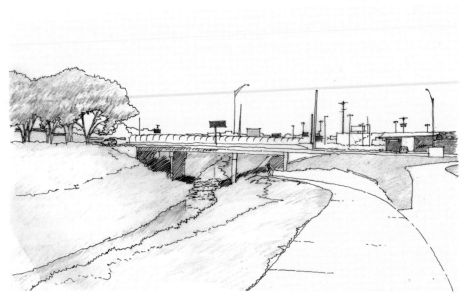

Figs. 8-1a and 8-1b: Omaha is a city of hills and creek valleys. The creek valleys could become a major asset for the community. A sketch of a creek in Omaha today and how it could look if creek waters were raised and the banks were landscaped.

Figs. 8-2a and 8-2b: Omaha has 1800 acres of public land along the edges of highways that could be landscaped to create a major change in the city's image.

parking ratios and the economics of parking mean that parking lots are inevitable. The perimeter of parking lots can be landscaped to screen the lots from adjacent roads and buildings, but it is also important to create some tree cover and green space within the lots themselves. Green parking lots can improve the local microclimate, and they can incorporate stormwater retention and filtration requirements that would otherwise need to be satisfied elsewhere on the property. Dealing with stormwater requirements makes the green parking lot more practical for developers than it may appear at first. Designing green parking lots in Omaha, where there can be heavy winter snowfalls, is more complicated than in places without much snow. Having trees in

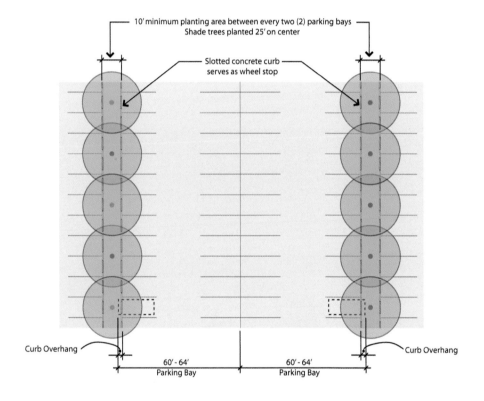

Fig. 8-3a: A green parking lot with pervious surfaces and subsurface detention areas can save developers land over separated stormwater detention areas otherwise likely to be needed. It is also possible to aggregate some of the planting at the periphery as long as the areas remain the same.

every other parking row, rather than between every row of cars, is a way of making it easier to plow a green parking lot. [Figures 8-3a and 8-3b]

SUBURBAN PARK PLAN

Omaha's Suburban Park Plan identifies appropriate park locations within each mile-square grid between the city's current boundaries and the limits where the city is permitted to annex. [Figure 8-4, page 116] As an identified piece of parkland becomes part of the city, it is set aside from whatever development includes it and the city's parks department assumes the maintenance. This policy preserves some of the areas that most need protection from development and relates parks to individual neighborhoods.

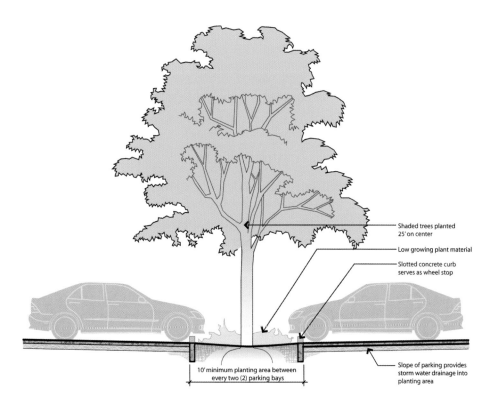

Fig. 8-3b: Section of planting strip for a green parking lot. It is also possible to use a five-foot planting strip, which would mean no net loss of parking spaces compared to a conventional parking lot. Over time, parking lot landscaping could transform the image of many parts of Omaha.

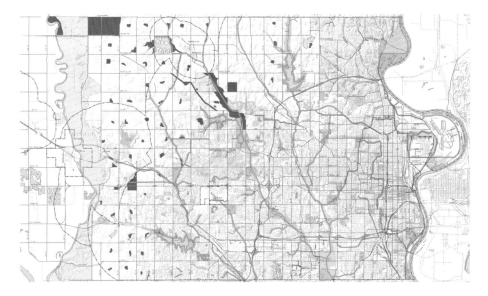

Fig. 8-4: Omaha's suburban park plan identifies green areas currently outside the city limits, at the left of the map, which will be set aside as parks when these areas are annexed.

CIVIC DESIGN

The areas of civic importance in the master plan, and in three overlay zoning districts, include Omaha's traditional downtown, but also the other parts of the city where the most people work, shop, or look for entertainment. The accompanying drawing of Omaha at night delineates these areas of civic importance, what downtown has become in the modern metropolitan city. [Figure 8-5] Among the requirements in the areas of civic importance overlay districts are building placement requirements in relation to principal streets and the use of green parking lots. Within the areas of civic importance are places where development needs more specific coordination and direction. The zoning will now permit the creation of civic place districts for such areas, as shown in the diagram for the area near the headquarters of Mutual of Omaha. [Figure 8-6, page 118]

Omaha has been requiring mixed use districts for commercial development in the newer parts of the city. The mix of uses and the higher intensity of development can make these districts the location for future transit stations. It is accepted that, in these highly accessible locations, buildings can't have the relationship to highways and major arterials that they do to downtown streets. However, on the internal streets in these mixed use developments an urban relationship of streets to buildings can be created. The diagram on page 119 shows buildings that meet the requirements of mixed use districts. [Figure 8-7]

Fig. 8-5: This drawing of Omaha at night delineates the areas of civic importance, what downtown has become in a modern metropolitan city.

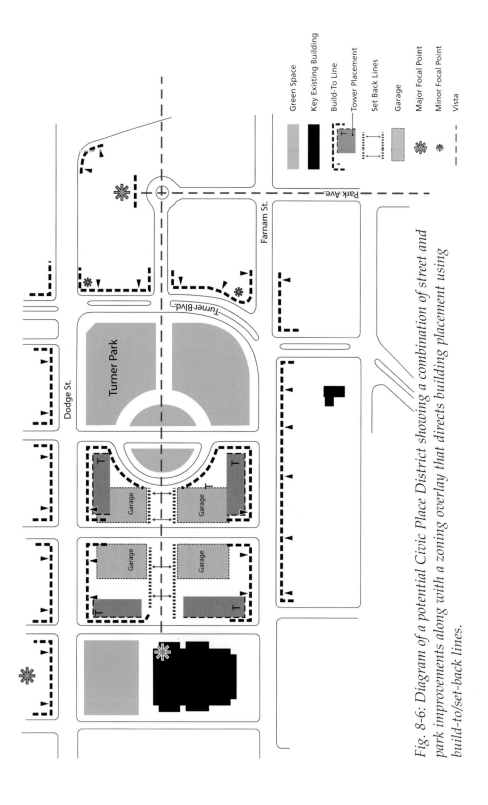

Fig. 8-6: Diagram of a potential Civic Place District showing a combination of street and park improvements along with a zoning overlay that directs building placement using build-to/set-back lines.

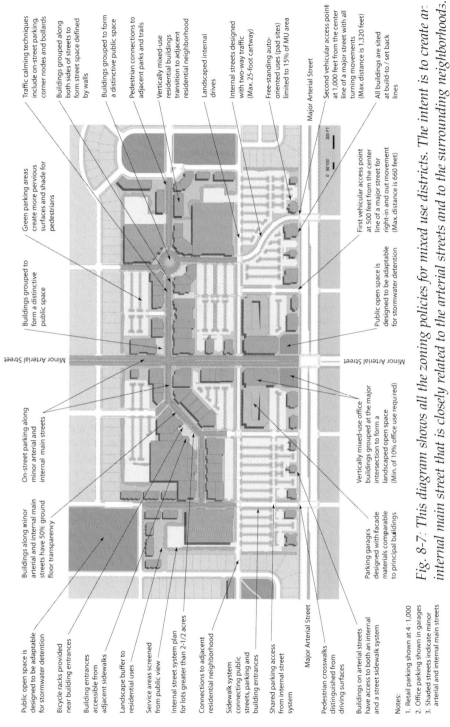

Fig. 8-7: This diagram shows all the zoning policies for mixed use districts. The intent is to create an internal main street that is closely related to the arterial streets and to the surrounding neighborhoods.

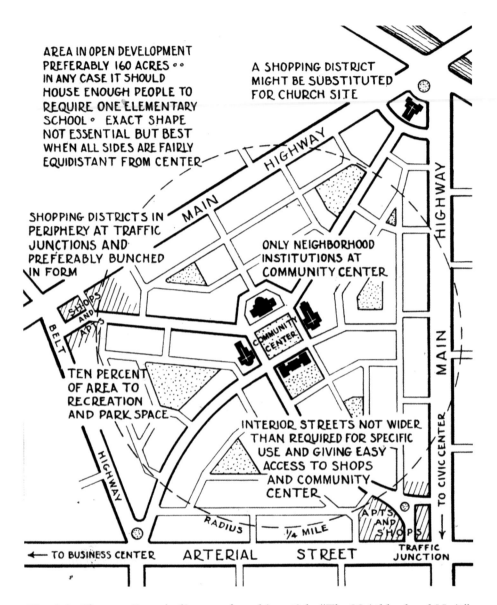

Fig. 8-8: Clarence Perry's diagram from his article "The Neighborhood Unit" in a volume of the 1929 Regional Plan of New York and its Environs. Perry defined a neighborhood as being contained within a circle with a quarter-mile radius, which is about a five-minute walking distance. Each Perry neighborhood is 160 acres—one-quarter of a square mile.

GUIDELINES FOR LARGE RETAIL BUILDINGS

Many of the attempts to improve large retail buildings by regulation turn out to be about architectural style. In Omaha an attempt is being made to deal with fundamentals, such as building massing, building placement, size and placement of signs, green parking lots, the position and landscaping of retaining walls, and other elements that actually have a bigger effect on the public than the design of the facades.

NEIGHBORHOOD DESIGN

One of the most widely accepted definitions of the neighborhood was published by Clarence Perry in a volume of the 1929 *Regional Plan of New York and its Environs.* Perry defined a neighborhood as being contained within a quarter-mile radius, which is about a five-minute walking distance. [Figure 8-8] That means that each neighborhood would be about 160 acres, one-quarter of a square mile. Perry suggested that the commercial districts should be located at intersections where they could serve four neighborhoods, and that institutions like churches and schools should be in the interior of the neighborhood, away from the busy commercial streets. The open land around Omaha is laid out on a mile-square grid, as it is around most U.S. cities. That means that each square mile (640 acres) can potentially contain four neighborhoods. [Figure 8-9]

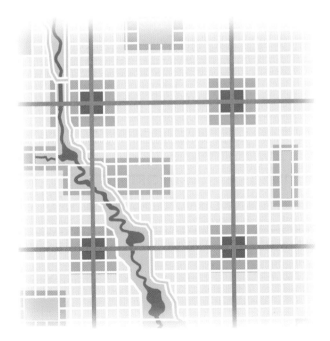

Fig. 8-9: Omaha's master plan locates commercial and mixed use centers at the intersection of major arterial streets, which occur every mile. With each square mile there is a park set aside by the Suburban Park Plan.

Omaha's master plan already designates the intersections of arterials as the most appropriate location for commercial development. The Suburban Park Plan already designates a park within each square mile. The result is that Omaha already has the basic elements of neighborhood development built in. [Figure 8-10] However, most new development within this framework takes the form of separate housing tracts and separate commercial development. It has not been conducive to neighborhood formation. What is missing in these developing parts of Omaha is a walkable environment that would tie all the newly built elements together into a neighborhood.

Fig. 8-10: With commercial or mixed use development every mile, and room within each square mile for four Clarence Perry neighborhoods, Omaha can insure that the framework for walkable new neighborhoods is present when the city annexes new territory.

WALKABLE RESIDENTIAL NEIGHBORHOODS

Much of the discussion about creating new neighborhoods involves traditional neighborhood design and images of front porches and picket fences. But the most important element of the traditional neighborhood is the ability to walk from one place to another. Next important is having a mix of housing types and sizes within the same neighborhood, although this was not always traditional. Development regulations need to deal with issues that are clearly in the public interest, like walkability, density, and connections to other districts. Front porches, architectural styles, and picket fences are best left to the individual developers or owners.

In the new Omaha zoning there is a walkable residential neighborhood district (WRN), which includes elements that enhance walkability and provides for a mix of housing types and sizes. This is a parallel code, as is the traditional neighborhood district (TND) code that has been enacted in other places. A developer can elect to use it, but is not required to. The incentive for the developer is the mix of housing types and lot sizes permitted, which is more flexible than conventional zoning. Some of the most critical provisions that promote walkability need to be in both the WRN and the subdivision ordinance, so they will promote walkable neighborhoods whether or not the developer elects to use the WRN district.

Requiring sidewalks is an obvious first step. Another element that promotes walkability is the maximum block perimeter, [Figure 8-11] which

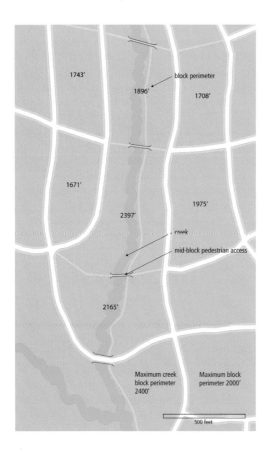

Fig. 8-11: One of the Walkable Residential Neighborhood Zone requirements is a maximum block size, so that pedestrian connections are maintained throughout the neighborhood.

makes it easier to find ways to walk through a neighborhood. Another is connectivity, which requires some streets to go through the neighborhood to other neighborhoods and to nearby commercial districts. Keeping streets pleasant and interesting is also important. Experience shows that minimizing the impact of garage doors and driveways on the street makes it more walkable, which leads to requirements to set garages back and keep driveways narrow when they reach their intersection with the street. Set-back garages and narrow driveways also make it easier to create continuous rows of street trees. A uniform set-back and build-to line is needed on both sides of the street to keep a good relationship between buildings and passersby.

A city in harmony with its green landscaped setting, and with walkable neighborhoods, civic places, and mixed use districts that are suitable destinations for public transit is part of the smart growth spectrum, which starts at transportation for the entire multi-city region and the preservation of regional open space.

NOTES

1.   The work described in this chapter was prepared for Omaha by Design and the City of Omaha by Wallace Roberts & Todd, LLC. Jonathan Barnett was the professional in charge, Ferdinando Micale was the project director, and Adam Krom and Yan Wang were among the key participants in the project for WRT. Brian Blaesser of Robinson and Cole was the advisor on implementation for the work leading to the adoption of the Urban Design Element of the Omaha Master Plan. The subsequent implementation study was lead by Brian Blaesser of Robinson & Cole, with WRT as a subconsultant. Steve Jensen, Omaha's Planning Director, Robert Peters, Omaha's former Planning Director, and Connie Spellman, Director of Omaha by Design, have played very important roles in this project, as has Del Weber who has chaired the advisory committee.

Jonathan Barnett wrote a more personal account of Omaha by Design for *Harvard Design Magazine*, spring/summer 2005, which was reprinted as a chapter of *Urban Planning Today*, edited by William S. Saunders, University of Minnesota Press, 2006.

9

America's Future and Federal Smart Growth Policies

W. Paul Farmer

Cities change. Economies change. Nations change. Environments change. Politicians are instrumental in setting the policies that guide change. The authors of this book have made compelling cases for smart growth as both a reaction to changes and as a key driver of future changes.

The premise of this book is that an increasingly competitive world requires the U.S. to become more efficient—smarter as a nation—if it is going to continue to prosper. A corollary is that the efficiency improvements must occur within the multi-city regions described in this book.

Smart growth, a successor to growth management, has been around since at least the early 1990s and embodies many of the principles of good planning that have been around for half a century or more.

Smart growth generally means more efficient use of land, mixed uses, transportation alternatives that reduce reliance on private automobiles, and better environmental stewardship. There must also be an equity component. How could growth without such a component ever be considered "smart"?

For a nation that consumes 25 percent of the world's oil, produces only five percent, and has only three percent of the world's known reserves, efficiency will be critical, and efficiency within these multi-city regions, or "supercities," is the key.

The U.S. is now running a balance of trade deficit that is seven percent of its GNP while economists consider three percent or more to be a dangerous level. If foreign investors start turning elsewhere, U.S. interest rates will rise, slowing the growth of our economy, particularly sectors such as housing that are especially sensitive to interest rates. In fact, worldwide investors are already looking elsewhere. Our current accounts flows—the difference between the foreign investments in the U.S. and U.S. investments abroad—turned negative in 2006. When was it last negative? Ninety years ago! This is big.

Yes, there are fundamental changes in our economic world. Of course, changes in our natural world are fundamental as well.

Scientists are no longer debating whether or not global warming is occurring. It is. They have also concluded that many human activities are key contributors.

First, the good news. Most of what can be done and needs to be done about this issue can be carried out by just 10 countries—the G8 plus China and India. These 10 are largely responsible for the problem and can fix it. Of course, the "fix" is to slow down the rate of increase of the harm that we are doing. That's the bad news—because the "fix" is extremely difficult to accomplish. Most credible scientists agree that sea levels are guaranteed to rise between three and eight feet within the next five decades, reaching levels last seen one million years ago. The rate of increase in carbon in the atmosphere began to change markedly in the 1970s. A 2006 NASA study calculates that our "do nothing" alternative could lead to a sea level rise of 80 feet, reaching levels not seen in three million years.

DUMB GROWTH

These are just two global changes—economic and environmental—that relate directly to domestic policy. Since U.S. domestic policies, from Lewis and Clark through the Great Society, have always come through an interplay of international and national forces, these global changes require fundamental changes in domestic policy if we are to remain a competitive nation.

Since the decades of the Great Depression and WWII, the interplay has both relied on and produced a domestic policy that has been consistent and effective. Social Security has given Americans confidence that their later years would be spent in dignity. Myriad housing policies created what is, arguably, the best housed people for any large country in history. Interstate highways ushered in the automobile age and increased personal mobility. Federal airport funding and military aircraft purchase did the same for the jet age. Federal water programs linked supplies with thirsty cities, often hundreds of miles apart, and later provided clean water for growing suburbs. Rural electrification brought power to farms and small towns.

Of course, this is an idealized picture of these policies and outcomes. Benefits were not equitably distributed, either spatially or among population groups. Racism too often was at play. But living standards were raised for a burgeoning middle class.

While the domestic policy of the first 150 years of our republic might be described by one word—decentralization—another word best describes our domestic policy of the last 75 years. That word is sprawl. Of course, the U.S never had a Presidential Commission on U.S. Settlement Patterns that recommended this policy choice. One wasn't needed. With 90/10 Interstate highway funding, interest deductions for home mortgages, water and sewer subsidies—the list could go on— a Great Society or Ownership Society tag for the whole lot of domestic policies was not required. In retrospect, they can be given such a tag: Dumb Growth.

In the 1950s we could be forgiven for our sprawl policies. For 20 years, beginning in 1929, the U.S. did not have a well-functioning domestic economy. First came the Depression, then the war. Overcrowding was rampant in the 1940s because housing demand far outstripped supply.

Today, most of these dumb growth policies remain intact. Dumb growth industries that learned how to make money under this system resist change. U.S. automakers cannot even figure out a profitable way to make cars. And some expect them to make state-of-the-art transit vehicles. Ford's bonds were rated "junk" in 2006. The market has spoken.

But the dumb growth industries, their ideologues, their apologists, and their very, very wealthy financiers continue to support the now discredited policies of the past.

SMART GROWTH

Smart growth requires entire new industries. The old ones are not likely to change quickly enough any more than the mainframe computer companies led the present computer revolution.

In addition to new industries, smart growth in a global economy requires several key federal policy changes.

First, the U.S. needs to get its energy policy right. It's apparent that the nation is not even close.

New production must be coupled with conservation and renewable sources, such as solar energy. Tax policies and incentives must be changed in a way that assures the markets of their longevity—and their ability to spur long-term investment. Without some degree of certainty, the private sector will not have enough confidence to make the required investments. Risk reduction requires long-term policy guarantees. Conservation must also be a key component. In Germany new homes use five percent of the energy consumed in a typical U.S. home.

Second, the U.S. needs to get its environmental policies right.

Many thought that the U.S. was on its way 35 years ago, and there have been many accomplishments. Air is cleaner. Wetlands are more protected, although the U.S. Supreme Court reduced those protections a bit in 2006. However, attacks on environmental laws are increasing, and it is clear that those laws will be overhauled. It is just a question of how that will occur and the substance of the changes that will emerge.

Third, the U.S. needs to get its infrastructure and transportation policies right.

This is about maintenance and choice. Repair first, then build in a way that increases choices.

Americans love choices but, today, most are very limited in their real transportation choices. In fact, most do not have any choice for most of their trips. The automobile is the only option. In the early 1990s, the U.S. could be rightfully proud of progress made through the enactment of the Intermodal Surface Transportation Efficiency Act (ISTEA), the most significant change in federal transportation policy in decades. APA was a key player in crafting those changes. Regression best describes the last two reauthorizations—TEA 21 (Transportation Equity Act for the 21st Century) and SAFETEA-LU (Safe, Accountable, Flexible, Efficient, Transportation Equity Act: A Legacy for Users)—in the face of lobbying by highway and related industries. During almost three years of debate over the most recent reauthorization, members of Congress were at least being honest in referring to the "highway bill."

Global competitiveness requires smart growth. It, in turn, can only be achieved if its proponents are far more prepared for the next surface transportation reauthorization effort, keeping in mind the fact that the bill needs to have support in 435 congressional districts. The dumb growth industries have shown that they understand the math.

Fourth, the U.S needs to get its hazard mitigation and disaster policies right.

People must again be protected. Local communities must assume more risk. No one should be paid to build in known hazard areas. Second homes are more likely to be built in hazard areas, yet the U.S. still provides a mortgage interest deduction for this type of construction. Essentially our federal government says, "We'll help you build where you shouldn't, we'll rescue you, and then we'll help you rebuild." Now, there's a dumb growth policy! The federal government should at least stop providing the interest deduction for second homes in known hazard areas and use those tax savings to capitalize a fund for housing after disasters. It could easily be made revenue neutral.

Here is the policy choice: Government can continue to help those who can afford a second home and choose to locate it in a known hazard area, or government can choose to help those with post-disaster housing needs. Hurricanes Katrina and Rita showed the glaring need; Congress must get equitable domestic policies in place.

Fifth, the U.S. needs to get its overall housing policies right.

The U.S. made a pledge of a decent home for all Americans in 1949. For a while, progress was being made. For the last 30 years, the U.S. has been withdrawing from that pledge. Withdrawal has been bipartisan. It is time to create new programs at the federal level so that state and local programs can be more effective. The private sector will provide most of the funds for affordable housing, but success cannot be achieved without significant new federal money and programs.

FREEDOM AND FAIRNESS

All of these new domestic policies need to be driven by basic American values of freedom and fairness.

Freedom. In *Whose Freedom?*, George Lakoff examines today's efforts by ideologues to redefine this most basic American idea to mean something it has never meant. He discusses property rights and suggests that someone's rights should be valued in a way that recognizes the collective creation of value through infrastructure investments. He suggests looking at the value of property in arid areas without publicly provided water. With arguably the best property system ever created, this is one area where radical reform is not needed. In fact, reform advocated by radical libertarians and developers will undermine our competitive position in a changing world.

Fairness. All Americans legitimately expect that their lives and those of their children will improve. Access to opportunities should not be blocked by mean-spirited laws. Cass Sunstein's "Radicals in Robes" documents efforts to radically change laws to benefit a few. This, too, undermines America's competitive advantage.

New domestic policies, founded on the values of freedom and fairness, need to be driven by economic efficiency and coordinated public-private investments as well. Canals, railroads, seaports, airports, and highways were built by government or government assistance. America cannot afford to fear building infrastructure in a smart growth, globally competitive way.

New domestic policies need to be driven by the values of stewardship. Gifford Pinchot, John Muir, Aldo Leopold, and Benton MacKaye all saw land as part of the national soul and knew that Americans must be stewards. Unfortunately, one of the failures of the last 75 years is that metropolitan regions were built around highways and sewer pipes rather than around natural systems. Continued growth requires change, and our new domestic policies must incorporate values of stewardship. Federal policies and programs must facilitate these efforts, not retard them.

In Pittsburgh some 20 years ago, an Indian from the Amazon rain forest visited while on a tour of U.S. cities to raise awareness of the shrinking forests. He said that all of the U.S. cities he had visited had destroyed the forests in order to build the cities. Pittsburgh was the first city he had found that had built the city within the forest. There is a good reason—Pittsburgh's geology makes it the most landslide-prone city in the U.S. The visitor would be disappointed were he to return today. Pittsburgh, a region of declining population, is destroying the forests of western Pennsylvania as it sprawls like any other region. Tax increment financing—a tool created for redevelopment—is now being used to level hillsides for big box retail stores.

Can the U.S. change? Can the U.S. really achieve a Smart Growth Domestic Policy, assuring its competitiveness and security?

The wealth of the nation today is a legacy of earlier decisions: National parks. The great Midwest, the breadbasket of the world. California, the fifth largest economy in the world.

The U.S. is not about to stop growing or stop building. Arthur C. Nelson (in the Autumn 2006 issue of the *Journal of the American Planning Association*) describes the magnitude and the nature of that growth. The demographics of the U.S. are undergoing tremendous changes. One of Nelson's many conclusions is that virtually all of the large lot homes needed over the next 25 years have already been built.

Seventy percent of the population growth and 80 percent of the job growth will be in our nine multi-city regions, the supercities of the future. How we add that growth will greatly influence our country's future competitiveness. These discussions will continue at APA's National Planning Conferences over the next four years in different multi-city regions, with conferences in Philadelphia, Las Vegas, Minneapolis, and New Orleans.

Berkeley planning professor Michael Tietz offered a comment at the annual planning educators' conference held in Fort Worth in 2006. The U.S. has had grand plans in the past but trends have always won out. What's new? Rapid and substantial population growth? No, the U.S. has had it and handled it. Rapid and substantial increases in people and goods moving about? No, that too has occurred and been handled. Teitz offered one new phenomenon: the rapid increases in the acreage that we consume per person. That's new.

Robert Yaro answered that we have implemented big plans before and cited railroads, highways, and parks. Two new phenomena can be added: increasing global competition and global warming. They meet Teitz's test: They are big and haven't been seen before.

China's cities are going to grow by 400 million to 600 million within 25 years. India, Malaysia, and Indonesia are growing as well. The world will build 1,200 new coal-fired power plants by 2050, 600 in China and 150 in the U.S. Coal, more than other fuel sources, produces greenhouse gases. Electricity lost in transmission increases several fold in suburban developments. Can we afford Dumb Growth Domestic Policies anymore?

Planners understand linkages. They take a longer view. They identify unexpected consequences.

Dumb Growth Domestic Policies are about to change. The U.S. simply does not control the global forces at play. The U.S. still has enormous influence, but it is increasingly shared. No longer a country of manifest destiny, the U.S must now live in a world where China is both its trading partner and its banker. The world may or may not be flat, but it has changed fundamentally.

The U.S. does control its domestic policies and these, too, must change fundamentally.

The rate of fundamental change in the world is increasing. The U.S., of necessity, *will* have a new domestic policy. Planners and smart growth advocates should play a major role in its creation.

Discussion Questions

1. In Chapter 1 Jonathan Barnett writes about a growth crisis that could be created both by increasing the U.S. population and by the nation's vibrant economy, high standard of living, rich natural resources, and abundant land. Why does he think that such favorable elements can help create a crisis?

2. In Chapter 3 Kaid Benfield writes about the runaway American Dream. What is running away and why does it compromise the dream?

3. Chapter 1 says that low-density urban sprawl is the normal U.S. growth pattern, deeply embedded in the official processes that fund and approve new development. What policies could change this pattern? Can individual planners and citizens help create these policies?

4. Not all parts of the country are growing at the same speed. Chapter 2 shows that much of the growth can be expected to take place in nine multi-city regions, some of them crossing state boundaries. More important, low-density growth patterns mean that far more fields and forests will be urbanized than is required by population increase alone. What do these projections tell us about planning for future growth in the U.S.?

5. Development in the U.S. is highly dependent on transportation by car and truck. Kaid Benfield tells us that gasoline consumption in the U.S. currently accounts for 11 percent of world energy production. Gasoline consumption is rising rapidly in India and China, as well as in other developing parts of the world. Will improvements in automotive technology cut energy consumption enough to make the highway-based transportation system sustainable in the U.S.?

6. Shelley Poticha in Chapter 4 writes that global competitors like Europe and Japan have multi-city regions, but they also have balanced transportation systems that include high-speed rail and local transit systems. Can the U.S. continue to be competitive without a similarly balanced transportation system?

7. Is it feasible to integrate high-speed rail and long-distance airline travel in the U.S.? What would be the advantages of doing this?

8. Shelley Poticha also points out that many more people than expected are using new urban rapid transit lines. If you commute by automobile, would you take transit instead if door-to-door trip times were similar and the transit system was comfortable and dependable?

9. A study of the seven-county Orlando region, described in Chapter 5, shows that growth around a balanced transportation system leads to far less loss of farmland and natural areas than accommodating the same population increase by continuing current development practice. The costs are also lower. Do you think such case studies are enough to convince people to change public policies?

10. In the case study of the Northeast Megalopolis, Robert Yaro and Armando Carbonell state that all projected population increases to 2050 could be accommodated within existing urbanized areas. However, to create this result, some growth would have to be diverted from "hot" development locations to bypassed areas that currently have a "cold" real estate market. Would it ever be feasible to do this? How could such a change be accomplished?

11. The destruction of much of New Orleans by hurricanes Katrina and Rita in 2005 points up the fact that many urban areas in the U.S. are vulnerable to natural disasters: not just hurricanes, but floods, earthquakes, and forest fires. Recovery in New Orleans is proceeding very slowly. Federal, state, and local government institutions seem unable to deal with destruction at this scale. Chapter 7 suggests a question: What would happen to the U.S. economy if a flood surge hit New York City and, simultaneously, a major earthquake hit Memphis and St. Louis?

12. Chapter 7 also deals with the possibility of worldwide rises in sea level as a result of climate change. What do scientific predictions tell us about growth management in coastal cities and in vacation areas along seashores?

13. Chapter 8 describes three components of smart growth: Green, Civic and Neighborhood. Many of the policies required can be shaped by local government. How well does your local government manage growth? Would any of the measures described in Chapter 8 be helpful in your community?

14. Paul Farmer in Chapter 9 summarizes changes in the global economy and the environment that should force the U.S. to shed its dumb growth domestic policies, and to create new growth policies based on freedom, fairness, and stewardship. He sees the federal government as essential in this process, because federal powers shape so much of current policy. What are the steps in the national political process that could bring about these changes, and how long do you think it will take to implement them? Alternatively, do you think the U.S. is doomed to lose its competitive economic advantages and degrade its environment because there is no political will to change?

Illustration Credits

Figures 2-1, 2-2, 2-3, and 2-4 courtesy of the University of Pennsylvania. Maps by Kyle Gradinger and Eric McAfee

Figure 3-1 courtesy NRDC, information from the Brookings Institution's Center for Urban and Metropolitan Policy

Figure 3-2 courtesy NRDC, information from the Surface Transportation Policy Project

Figure 3-3 courtesy NRDC, data from U.S. Department of Energy

Figure 3-4 courtesy NRDC, information from *Sustainability and Cities* by Peter Newman and Jeffrey Kenworthy

Figure 4-1 courtesy of the Federal Railroad Administration

Figure 4-2 courtesy of the California High-Speed Rail Authority

Figure 4-3 courtesy of the Texas High Speed Rail and Transportation Corporation (THSRTC)

Figure 4-4 courtesy of the Midwest Interstate Passenger Rail Commission

Figures 4-5, 4-6 courtesy of the Center for Neighborhood Technology

Figures 5-1 through 5-11 courtesy of the University of Pennsylvania

Figures 6-1 through 6-6 courtesy of the University of Pennsylvania

Figures 7-1 courtesy of Wallace Roberts & Todd, LLC

Figure 7-2 map courtesy of Wallace Roberts & Todd, LLC, information from the City of New York

Figures 7-3, 7-4 maps courtesy of Wallace Roberts & Todd, LLC, based on information from the USGS

Figures 8-1a through 8-11 courtesy of Wallace Roberts & Todd, LLC—except Figure 8-8, which is courtesy of the Regional Plan Association

Index

137

About the Authors

Jonathan Barnett, FAIA, FAICP is a Professor of Practice in City and Regional Planning and director of the Urban Design Program at the University of Pennsylvania. He has been an urban design consultant to many cities, including Charleston, Cleveland, Kansas City, Nashville, New York City, Norfolk, Omaha, Philadelphia and Pittsburgh. He is the author of *Redesigning Cities*, published by Planners Press, and many other books and articles.

F. Kaid Benfield is the senior attorney and director of the Smart Growth Program of the Natural Resources Defense Council in Washington, D.C. He is a founder and former vice chair of Smart Growth America. His numerous publications include *Solving Sprawl* (2001) and *Once There Were Greenfields* (1999).

Armando Carbonell, AICP, is a senior fellow and cochair of the Department of Planning and Urban Form at the Lincoln Institute of Land Use Policy in Cambridge, Massachusetts. He is also a visiting professor at the University of Pennsylvania.

W. Paul Farmer, FAICP, is the executive director and CEO of the American Planning Association, with offices in Chicago, Illinois, and Washington, D.C. He was previously the executive director of Planning and Development in Eugene, Oregon, the Director of Planning in Minneapolis, and Pittsburgh's deputy planning director.

Shelley Poticha is president and CEO of Reconnecting America and of the Center for Transit Oriented Development, both headquartered in Oakland, California. She was formerly the executive director of the Congress for the New Urbanism.

Robert D. Yaro is president of the Regional Plan Association in New York City. He is also a Professor of Practice in City and Regional Planning at the University of Pennsylvania.